S0-BDS-726

Mary Casanova and YOU

Recent Titles in
The Author and YOU Series
Sharron McElmeel, Series Editor

Gerald McDermott and YOU
Jon C. Stott, Foreword and Illustrations by Gerald McDermott

Alma Flor Ada and YOU, Volume I
Alma Flor Ada

Jim Aylesworth and YOU
Jim Aylesworth and Jennifer K. Rotole

Toni Buzzeo and YOU
Toni Buzzeo

Jacqueline Briggs Martin and YOU
Jacqueline Briggs Martin with Sharron L. McElmeel

Bob Barner and YOU
Bob Barner

Mary Casanova and YOU

Mary Casanova

The Author and YOU

Sharron L. McElmeel, Series Editor

LIBRARIES
UNLIMITED
A Member of the Greenwood Publishing Group

Westport, Connecticut · London

Library of Congress Cataloging-in-Publication Data

Casanova, Mary.
Mary Casanova and you / Mary Casanova.
    p. cm. — (Author and you)
  Includes bibliographical references and index.
  ISBN 1-59158-405-1 (pbk : alk. paper)
    1. Casanova, Mary—Juvenile literature. 2. Authors, American—20th
century—Biography—Juvenile literature. 3. Children's literature—
Authorship—Juvenile literature. I. Title.
PS3553.A78962Z46   2007
813'.54—dc22   2006033681
[B]

British Library Cataloguing in Publication Data is available.

Copyright © 2007 by Mary Casanova

All rights reserved. No portion of this book may be
reproduced, by any process or technique, without the
express written consent of the publisher.

Library of Congress Catalog Card Number: 2006033681
ISBN: 1-59158-405-1

First published in 2007

Libraries Unlimited, 88 Post Road West, Westport, CT 06881
A Member of the Greenwood Publishing Group, Inc.
www.lu.com

Printed in the United States of America

The paper used in this book complies with the
Permanent Paper Standard issued by the National
Information Standards Organization (Z39.48–1984).

10 9 8 7 6 5 4 3 2 1

Cover images:

Cover from *Wolf Shadows* by Mary Casanova. Cover art © 1997 by
Dan Brown. Hyperion Paperbacks for Children. Used with permission.

Cover from *Riot* by Mary Casanova. Cover art © 1998 by
Eric Velasquez. Cover design by Stephanie Bart-Horvath.
Hyperion Paperbacks for Children. Used with permission.

Cover from *Moose Tracks* by Mary Casanova. Cover art © 1995 by
Kam Mack. Cover design by Stephanie Bart-Horvath. Hyperion
Paperbacks for Children. Used with permission.

Cover from *When Eagles Fall* by Mary Casanova. Cover art © 2002 by
Wendell Minor. Hyperion Books for Children. Used with permission.

3 0002 00092769 9

Contents

Series Foreword

Have you ever wanted to sit down and talk with the author of a beloved story? Have you ever wanted to find out more? Good authors are like good friends. They touch our hearts and minds. They make us wonder, and they make us want to learn.

When young readers become engaged with story, they invariably ask questions.

- Why is Gerald McDermott so fascinated with myths and legends? How did he locate and choose which stories he wished to retell? Are the images in his books faithful to the culture they represent?
- Did Alma Flor Ada know the people we meet in her stories? Where does she come from? Why does she write in Spanish and English?
- Can Toni Buzzeo tell us how much of the Sea Chest is legend and what part is fact? What character does she like best: the Dawdle Ducking, Papa Loon? How does she get her ideas?

As teachers and librarians, we know that the moment children begin asking questions, we are presented with a wonderful opportunity. In response, we may hold discussions or create learning activities. Yet answers to some questions are hard to come by. After all, we and our students cannot just sit down and talk with the authors we love and admire. But wouldn't it be great if we could?

Libraries Unlimited has developed *The Author and YOU* series to give you the next best thing to a real-life visit with your favorite children's authors and illustrators. In these books, you'll hear from authors and illustrators as they reflect on their work and explain to YOU, the reader, what they really had in mind. You'll find answers to some of the questions you and your students might ask, and to some you never thought to ask.

Just as each author or illustrator is a unique individual, so will his or her conversation with YOU be unique and individual. There is no formula, no predesigned structure. We've simply asked authors or illustrators to discuss the things they think are important or interesting about themselves and their books—and to share their comments with YOU.

Some authors will provide actual ideas and plans for you to use in sharing books with young readers. Others will share ideas that will help you generate your own ideas and connections to their work. In some cases, the author writes the book in collaboration with another. In others, it is a private reflection; but in all cases you'll discover some fascinating information, and come away with valuable insights.

It is our hope that by giving you these special messages from authors and illustrators, *The Author and YOU* series will increase your joy and understanding of literature—and, in turn, will help YOU motivate young readers, surround them with literacy and literacy activities, and share the joy of understanding.

This volume in *The Author and YOU* series, by Mary Casanova, joins those previously authored by Gerald McDermott, Alma Flor Ada, Toni Buzzeo, Jim Aylesworth, Jacqueline Briggs Martin, and Bob Barner. Mary Casanova is an author of picture books and novels for older readers. Her award-winning picture books include *The Hunter* (illustrated by Ed Young) and *Some Dog!* (illustrated by Ard Hoyt). Casanova enjoys the outdoors and lives near the Canadian border in Ranier, Minnesota. Her books often present challenges in nature and focus on relationships between people and the environment. Her most recent books, middle grade novels, include *Jess*, a book promoted by American Girl as their "Girl of the Year" (2006) and a series called Dog Watch, from Simon and Schuster. We are excited to present Mary Casanova's perspective on her life and writing.

Sharon Coatney
Sharron McElmeel

"Our lives are like fireflies, brilliant flashes of light in the darkness, here and gone. Each life matters. Listen to your dreams and giftings; take risks, live fully, make a difference."

Mary Casanova, as quoted from an author
profile by Sharron McElmeel.

Credit: From the archives of Sharron McElmeel. Reprinted with permission.

Introduction

Writing about my life is like gathering laundry, fresh from the dryer, and setting it on the street corner for others to see. I mean, who wants to examine another person's laundry? Yet it's an honor to be asked to share my path as a children's author. And so, as awkward and self-conscious as this process is, I'll begin. Going through darks, lights, and whites. Folding. Tossing out threadbare items. Trying to match socks. Maybe you'll be able to stand back and make some sense of it all, see patterns, or draw your own insightful conclusions. Maybe you'll find some small thing. A button, perhaps. A stray sock that matches one of yours. If so, take what you find useful. After all, we're all just passing through.

Mary in 2006. Reprinted with permission.

* * *

Age two at Elbow Lake cabin with family pet, Stormy. Credit: From Gazelka family albums. Reprinted with permission.

From dawn to dusk, my childhood home on the outskirts of St. Paul, Minnesota, hummed with the chatter and activities of *two* sisters and *seven* brothers. We had pets of every kind, from gerbils to goats to horses. Our backyard was Lake Johanna, where we skated in winter and swam in summer. Surrounded by water, wildlife, and fields, I spent plenty of time outdoors, finding adventure and benefiting from my parents' benevolent neglect. In many ways, it seemed the ideal childhood.

Coming from such a big family, however, I was imprinted with being *one-of-ten*, which for me meant an overriding sense of voicelessness, invisibility, and a need to be heard. Moreover, I was a reluctant reader who had a hard time following directions and concentrating (and these days would likely be diagnosed with having ADD, attention deficit disorder). My teachers often remarked on my report cards: "Mary's a good student, but she fails to live up to her true potential."

Family portrait at Lake Johanna home in St. Paul, Minnesota. Mary, grade eight (back row, far right). Credit: From Gazelka family album. Reprinted with permission.

My success as a children's author comes as a huge surprise to me—and brings with it new challenges. I've had to overcome panic attacks and a debilitating fear of speaking. I've learned to present to auditorium-filled audiences of kids of all ages and to hold their attention. Though I recently sold my twentieth book, I still get rejection letters and I've had to learn how to pack quickly—so as not to miss the next plane, since my books have taken me as far away as France, Belgium, Norway, and Belize.

A decade after the launch of my first novel, I never tire of hearing that my books turn reluctant readers into avid readers; that the issues in my novels make for great classroom discussions with kids begging for the next chapter; that a three-year-old wants to hear one of my picture books over and over. For me, though, the greatest satisfaction is venturing into the unknown, listening to the story that calls my name, and sitting down to that blank page to begin again.

After all, that's what writers do.

Taking a break after a full day of school presentations in Kalispell, Montana. Credit: From the archives of Mary Casanova. Reprinted with permission.

PART ONE

A Writer's Life

Growing Up

My earliest memory is riding in a shopping cart, legs dangling, as my mom pushed the cart through the aisles of Foodtown. I was no more than two or three, but I discovered that when I smiled at other shoppers, they smiled back. I had learned something important about human nature and a real-life lesson in "reaping what you sow." Was this the start of my becoming a writer? I doubt it. But it does remind me that at an early age I was an observer of others and was innately curious about the world around me.

I made my debut on Groundhog Day, February 2, 1957, in Duluth, Minnesota. Born fourth to my family, we moved in my first year to the suburbs of St. Paul.

My parents worked at making their children's lives better than what they had each experienced during the Depression on the Iron Range of Minnesota. My father, Gene Gazelka, grew up an only child in a Polish-Norwegian Catholic household. His father was a house painter and violinist. To help keep food on the table, my dad—as a boy—peddled newspapers and raised, trained, and sold white rats. And when World War II broke out, he enlisted.

When my dad returned from the Navy, he married my mother, Joyce Anderson, Queen of the Letterman's Ball at the junior college. My mother grew up in a hard-working family of Swedish and Finnish descent who "never hugged and never said 'I love you' or gave compliments.'" When her father worked on the railroads, she helped put up hay with her sister at their small farm at Mud Lake, Minnesota.

When she wasn't tending the chickens or caring for cows, she loved to explore the outdoors. In winter, she hiked with her wooden skis to the top of the nearest slopes

Age two, in the dress my mother sewed for me. Credit: From Gazelka family album. Reprinted with permission.

and loved skiing down again. Intelligent and creative, she dreamed of becoming an architect, but after a year-and-a-half of college, she married and began a family—with ten children. Though she never finished college, she managed over the years to design, draft, and contract numerous remodeling projects and two family cabins.

My parents loved God, family, and nature—and I do believe in that order. Every Sunday we piled into the station wagon to attend mass at St. John's Catholic Church in New Brighton, Minnesota. As a child, I always wore a dress to church with white patent leather shoes and a lace covering pinned on my head (or a hat). That's when the masses were conducted in Latin, which I definitely didn't understand. But I wanted to be devout, nonetheless. Before I could read, I moved my forefinger across the lines in the devotional, pretending to follow along. When I made my first communion, I walked up the aisle with my hands together, fingertips pointed heavenward, just like a nun. Before long the church evolved to English masses and guitar music.

As much as they tried to instill spiritual values in their kids, my parents were equally firm believers in God's creation: Nature. Several times a year they packed us up and headed to northern Minnesota to spend time

Two years old and riding high in the arms of Grandpa Pete after mass. Credit: From Gazelka family albums. Reprinted with permission.

My parents, Gene and Joyce Gazelka, married for fifty-seven years Credit: From Gazelka family album. Used with permission.

with both sets of grandparents at their cabins: one cabin was on Elbow Lake, which we could reach only by boat, and the other cabin was on Eagles Nest Lake, offering more modern amenities. I learned from my delicious weeks at these cabins to love the north woods. The scent of pines, spruce, and cedar wafted in the cabin windows. Every morning I woke to the sound of white-throated sparrows that seemed to call my name. I fished, swam, rowed, canoed, hiked, picked blueberries, weathered thunderstorms and raids by errant black bears, braved spidery outhouses, and listened to stories around the campfire.

At the Elbow Lake cabin, situated on a south-facing cove with amber water and golden sand, I soaked up the heat of the sauna, loved the sizzle of water on hot rocks, and felt reborn after jumping off the dock into the cold lake. How can I describe the taste of my Grandma Fannie's blueberry pancakes, hot off the griddle on her wood-fired cookstove? How can I convey the slap of cards at the table, Grandpa Eric's accordion playing, the creak of that red rocking chair, the whir of dragonfly wings as they hatched by the hundreds from their watery beetle shells and took flight? As writers, we try to convey our sense of the world through words, but to me, my efforts fall short. Writing, however, is the closest I can come to recreating what moves me, whether from the past or today or in my imagination.

In a big family, older kids read to younger kids. Susan, age seven (left), reading to Paul, age three, and Mary, age five. Credit: From Gazelka family albums. Reprinted with permission.

Mary, age six, before diving underwater on "the back of a mighty whale," her dad. Credit: From Gazelka family albums. Reprinted with permission.

My other grandparents, Grandpa Pete and Grandma Dolly, offered a different cabin experience on Eagles Nest Lake. Their half-log-sided cabin boasted electricity, indoor plumbing, and flower boxes filled with plastic flowers. I laughed at Grandpa Pete's antics—telling jokes that would send his false teeth flying; playing his fiddle as he danced across the frayed wool carpet; and refereeing his instigated "all-star wrestling" matches with my siblings. In the evenings, we sang and danced to thick records on the old record player. And during the day, we fished from my grandparents' ancient wooden cruiser.

Like my Grandpa Pete, my dad was a storyteller and jokester. He loved to tell stories and make people laugh. He had a way of unifying any audience through stories, whether of wildlife encounters, tall tales, or jokes. His warm-hearted storytelling served him well at home and at work. At home, no matter how frustrated my mom would get, he could always get her to laugh or smile. And he took this storytelling ability with him through his career with State Farm Insurance, where he largely worked as a manager.

He also could be headstrong, following his gut and not always listening to the opinions of others. When our growing family needed more space, he returned one day to tell my mom that he'd found a house just down the road on Lake Johanna. "On a lake?" My mother was very interested.

"It's ours," he told her. He'd bought it without her having stepped a foot on the property.

When we moved in, my mother stepped into the kitchen and opened a cupboard, only to see a fat rat peering back at her. Despite her initial anger with my father's impulsiveness, the Lake Johanna home—once a convalescent home for sick children at the turn of the century—became her favorite home over the years. With six bedrooms and a little remodeling, plus several surrounding acres of land, it gave our family room to grow.

Whether at home or at a cabin, my mom was my role model for appreciating life's simple gifts and for paying attention to everyday miracles. At our home on the outskirts of St. Paul, I would often hike up our long driveway from school and find my mother in her flower gardens. "Come here, Mary," she'd say. "Just take a look at the colors inside this tulip!" It was her openness to life—with all its colors, scents, and textures—that taught me to pay attention and to wonder. After all,

Despite the work of raising a big family, my parents enjoyed time together. Credit: From Gazelka family albums. Reprinted with permission.

what writer can write if she doesn't draw on the basic ingredients of life in all its grit and dust and rainbow hues?

Perhaps it was my parents' love of nature that made them say "yes" over and over and over again to pets. There was Stormy, who birthed heroic litters of black Lab puppies. And the rabbit hutch my dad built with baby bunnies snuggled in their den lined by their mother's soft, downy hairs.

Our least friendly pet was a Canadian goose who guarded his harem of white geese fiercely, often leaving welts on our legs from his wings or beak. And there were goats, which stunk so badly we sold them and upgraded to horses. And the poor kitten I biked home with from the pet store in a brown paper bag over my handlebar—to which my parents said yes. And Rojo, a red Irish setter. And goldfish, gerbils, hamsters, guinea pigs, and a passel of wild birds that my oldest brother, Mark, raised in large pens. All this—this *children's zoo atmosphere*—enlarged my creativity. In my writing career, I have often chosen animals as subject matters or woven them into my stories to soften the subject matter (dogs in *Curse of a Winter Moon* and *Riot*, for example). If our interests lead us in part to what we write about, then it's no surprise that my childhood helped steer me toward animals—from horses to dogs, from wolves to otters.

We moved to our rambling two-story lake home the summer I was between fourth and fifth grades. It was a summer that marked the end of my early childhood years and the loss of my childhood best friend, Carol Keiser.

Carol and I had been childhood friends since we were one-year-olds. She lived on the other side of the white board fence that divided our yards. Her house was yellow; ours was robin's egg blue. We napped at each other's homes, and I still remember the lilting sound of her bedroom's cotton curtains breathing in and out against the screened windows as we drifted to sleep. We roamed from her home to mine and back again. Sandwiches at her home were made of homemade

A childhood filled with pets. Mary at five with a favorite bunny. Credit: From Gazelka family albums. Reprinted with permission.

whole wheat bread (before it was known to be healthy). At my house, I loved sandwiches on white processed bread. We never fought, but shared our early years in easy companionship. Though I had sisters, they were older and only remotely interested in spending time with me. So Carol became my best friend—and my home away from home.

All the years I knew her, her haircut stayed the same: short, silky, brown hair with bangs. I see her smiling openly, without judgment, as we ventured from my rabbit hutch to her new swing set glider. I remember our igloo snow fort we carved from deep, towering snowdrifts. And the fort held our secrets in its icy blue walls (much like a scene I depict in *The Klipfish Code* between two girlfriends).

Our friendship was untroubled and generous. One late August day as we played croquet in her yard, chasing colorful wooden balls around our little course, I happened to stand behind her (stupidly) as she swung her croquet mallet. Her windup was powerful, and I lost half of a front tooth. I raced home crying, cupping my mouth in my hands, blood spewing over my shorts. Later that day, when I returned from the dentist with a capped tooth, Carol had left me a brand-new sand pail, shovel, and sand sifter. But I heard she felt so terrible that I marched right over and gave it to her to cheer her up.

Then Carol's family moved to Ohio, and I moved down the street, and I felt the soft closing of a childhood door behind me. A new phase was about to begin, one that I would call "a five-year wandering in search of self." I filled up my initial loneliness by making friends with Becky, who lived a bike ride away. Becky imitated her older sister by smoking, drinking, and swearing. I'm not sure what drew me, but I knew I was desperately in need of a friend. In her basement, we'd listen to her older sister's records. But it wasn't a real friendship, and after a falling-out between us (I don't remember over what), I stepped off the school bus steps one morning and her older sister pushed me down. I picked myself up off the sidewalk with skinned knees and a bruised heart, and started another day of school.

At home, life bubbled with responsibility and play, with an emphasis on the latter. Every Saturday morning, my mom set a list of chores on the dining room table and we took turns picking the most appealing task. I cleaned the bathrooms, vacuumed the living room, washed windows, and folded endless loads of laundry, which I put in appropriate piles on a double row of long shelves labeled *Dad, Mom, Sherry, Mark, Susan, Mary, Paul, Brian, Greg, Jim, Peter,* and *Todd.* When I finished my chores, I was free to play, unless I needed to help make sandwiches first (a dozen at a time) or change a diaper (one of my brothers was always in diapers).

Growing up in a big family means not developing a strong sense of boundaries—what's yours, what's mine, and what's in between. If someone took my toothbrush, I took the nearest and newest-looking toothbrush in the toothbrush holder. If I was in the bathroom washing my face early before school and forgot to lock the door, one of my little brothers often wandered in. More than once, while I was standing at the sink and a short distance from the toilet, warm pee hit my leg from a half-asleep little brother.

Most of the time I shared a bedroom with my older sister Susan, who drew a line down our double bed with her fingernail and insisted I not cross over the line or risk getting clawed. We took turns singing to Beatles music in front of the mirror. She told me, "I like Paul and John; that means you can only like George or Ringo."

I replied, "I don't have to like them. I like Paul best!"

"No! You can't!"

I believe I spit in her face.

She clawed my arms (she really could grow her nails long, which I have never been able to do.)

That in turn brought tears and screams, and we both ended up getting a spanking by our dad, which meant that he took his belt off and used it to spank us a few times on our rumps. Having three older siblings, I learned to avoid most of these punishments by being "nice" and avoiding confrontation, something I would have to learn to undo in adulthood, since conflict by itself isn't bad, but how you handle it.

In fifth grade, I wanted to hang out with my sister and her friend Britta. "Go home!" Susan shouted from her bike. But, desperate to be included, I pressed on behind them on my blue bicycle. "I mean it!" she shouted, stopping on the gravel driveway. She charged over, wrestled me off my bike, and then tossed my bike into the weeds and took off with her friend. Did I listen to her need for space with her friend? Hardly! All I knew was what I wanted and needed, and in my big family, getting your needs met often meant being relentlessly persistent. Now, as an adult, I might call it obnoxious. I think I know better now. Not until we were nearly adults did Susan and I get along very well. Now we're great friends.

Sherry, my oldest sister and the firstborn in our family, was seven years older than me. I looked up to her with her foxlike eyes and silky dark hair. A fine artist, she captured lions, horses, and deer with her paintbrush. And she was the first of our family to go to college. I remember heading off with my parents and my sister to get Sherry moved into her dorm. In the hallway, my dad happened to lean against the wall and suddenly a fire alarm went off, sending students fleeing! When I glanced back, I noticed that his shoulder had broken the alarm bell. In response, we hurried back to our car, said good-bye to my sister, and headed home.

Mark, my older brother, should have been a stand-up comic. He nicknamed everyone in the family. The nicknames were:

Sherry, the oldest: "Kowabunga" or "La Casa"

Susan: "Sauce," which started out as Carcass, but evolved to something a little kinder.

Me: "Culla," which in its original was Culla Moiaka. Why such a name? Well, according to Mark, Culla is Finnish for fish and Moiaka is Finnish for stew, though I do not vouch for the spelling or authenticity on these words.

Paul: "Coma," because Paul slept in late so many mornings that he often, according to Mark, appeared to be in a coma. Paul was also known as King Coma.

Brian: "Chips," short for Buffalo Chips, but my mom protested, so it was shortened to something kinder—sort of.

Greg: "Gorsky," a shortened version of Gregorski.

Jim: "Jimbo"

Peter: "Skovich," from the lengthier version: Petroskovich. Who knows?

Todd: Whitey, because of his white-blond hair.

Mark's self-proclaimed nickname was "Prophet," which, amazingly, stuck for years but has been recently challenged by his blue-eyed toddling niece, Lydia, who thought he should be called "Uncle Beandip." This new nickname is sweet revenge for the rest of us, and in the back of my mind, a novel might be brewing by that very title.

Every night, tired from playing outdoors—swimming, water-skiing, sailing, horseback riding, roaming and wandering, biking, playing war in the fields and swamp, sliding down the steep hill toward the lake, playing hockey on the frozen lake—we gathered at the sound of the gong. The gong was a triangle of heavy steel, made by my Grandpa Eric, which my mom clanged with a steel rod. The rhythmic gonging rang out across the fields and water and called us all in for supper.

We sat at an oak table with three leaves, held hands, and said grace together—"Bless us, Oh Lord, for these thy gifts which we are about to receive. From thy bounty, through Christ our Lord. Amen." Then we dove in, arguing about whether to pass to the left or the right. The table was always filled with food: baked chicken and mashed potatoes, beef stew, corn on the cob and hamburgers, salads, and desserts. Every mealtime, at least one person spilled a glass of milk, which brought cheering. We rotated doing dishes in teams of two, and when it was my night to do supper dishes, it meant at least an hour or two in the kitchen before the job was finished.

Though I was surrounded by nine siblings at home, when I left for school each day, I was on my own. I never climbed aboard the same school bus with my siblings or attended the same schools at the same time. This strikes me as a stark contrast to my family life, where I was in the middle of a large pack, yet almost like an only child when I went off to school. My older sisters and brother had gone to a Catholic school, and my parents opted to send the rest of us to public school. The thing about a big family is I always wanted more attention—from my parents, siblings, anyone—than I seemed to receive. If I disappeared for hours at a time, no one knew. If I was running a fever, I needed to tell my mom, as she wouldn't likely notice on her own. And so I spent my life wanting the stage lights to shine on me, and I suspect this is true for most kids from big families. However, to my surprise, whenever attention came my way, when I found myself answering a question in class, performing a bit part in a skit or onstage, I suffered panic attacks. I had no idea how to handle the spotlight if it passed my way. And maybe that tug-of-war between needing to be seen, yet cringing at being truly visible, explains my often erratic behavior in my elementary school years.

The playgrounds of Ralph R. Reader Elementary were smack-dab between the one-level brick school and the drive-in theater (where I would later go on dates in high school). I tried out several identities in my later elementary years: boy chaser, bus-patrol good student, cool kid and soft-bully, and occasional friend to the outcast. Mostly, I remember feeling desperate to fit in. I'd walk home with Leslie from fifth grade and smoke cigarette butts on our way back to school. I'd be friendly with Bonnie, who had carrot-colored hair unkempt as a squirrel's nest, and who always carried a sharp, pungent smell like never-washed athletic socks. I wanted to be as good as the saints I heard about at church. And in my need to be popular and to push the boundaries, I wanted to flirt with being bad, too. I went right along with a bullying prank on the bus. And the prank was aimed at Justin, who looked steadfastly forward through his dark-rimmed glasses; Justin, who tended to use four-syllable words and knew too many answers to teachers' questions; Justin, who was probably one of the most gifted students in our sixth grade class.

Scott talked me into the plan, and I was happy to be included because Scott was charismatic, cute, and funny. He dressed sporty, savvy even, for his age. He carried himself with impish, appealing confidence. "Mary, tomorrow, sit down on the bus next to Justin and pretend you really like him. Then, when he seems comfortable, we'll be sitting behind him and put icicles down his back."

I wish, I wish I had said no. I wish I hadn't been a pushover for what seemed popular. I wish I had spared Justin. But I didn't. I was caught up in the fun, the plan, the scheme for mischief. And sadly, the plan worked. Justin believed I was being genuinely friendly, and when his shoulders relaxed, Scott and another friend put a large icicle down Justin's back. Justin jumped up, his face reddening, and tried to hit at the other boys, but his swats only looked pathetic. I moved to sit somewhere else, sick at what I'd just done. And Justin never forgave me—even years later at a class reunion—even as an adult, he carried resentment toward me for the pain I'd caused him. And ever since that day, I've carried regret.

And that's all part of learning.

Through moments such as those, I figured out who I was—and who I wasn't. When Vickie suggested shoplifting, I biked right along for the adventure, only to find that removing a pack of gum from the candy counter carried an impossibly heavy weight of guilt. The next day, I returned to the store on my bike and left a quarter on the shelf from where I'd stolen the gum. I wasn't a shoplifter. I didn't want to ever do that again. That wasn't the kind of adventure I'd hoped to find.

Increasingly, I found myself feeling true to myself when I was outdoors and being active. I was true to myself when I water-skied, steadying those big water skis against the pull of the boat, hanging on for dear life until I "popped" out of the water and soared atop the boat's wake. I was true to myself when I swam off the pontoon boat, playing tag for hours with my siblings, enchanted by the amber watery world between the pontoons—the best place to hide. I was true to myself when I downhill-skied with my friend Mike, who also taught me to sail, and found I loved both sports. I was true to myself when I played the piano—not in practicing lessons necessarily, but when I sat down to hear the notes I was playing and enjoyed creating music ... when I felt the notes in "Moon River" or melodies from my favorite musicals—*Camelot* and *The Sound of Music*. And I was most certainly true to myself atop the back of my horse. I felt alive, real, and I began to pay attention to such moments.

Somehow, I survived the late '60s, early '70s, and Johanna Junior High School in those "wandering" years. I kept a diary and wrote

Any piano was an opportunity to play. Credit: From Gazelka family albums. Reprinted with permission.

about square dancing with the cutest boys in my gym class. Little did I know that I would one day marry one of my diary entries: Charlie Casanova. And it was the summer between sixth and seventh grades that I had my first girl-boy beach party. Another girlfriend, Mary K., who was much more astute about all things social, put together an "invite" list. A dozen kids showed up for an evening of swimming from the pontoon boat, roasting hot dogs, and chatting around the bonfire. Again, on that initial list: Charlie Casanova. Not until we were both in college at the University of Minnesota, however, would we begin taking a serious interest in one another.

School wasn't difficult for me academically, but what student goes through junior high without wincing with self-consciousness? Miss Peterson, my eighth grade English teacher, thought for some reason that it would be good for each student to memorize a popular song and lip-sync before the class (this was before the word "karaoke" was around). "And it would be especially nice," she said, "if you dance while you're singing." Why she thought this would benefit us in some way, I have no idea. It was the most painful moment of my whole year. I chose a song with the refrain "Just call me angel of the morning," which I didn't understand, and I used the tips I'd gotten from my older sister on how to dance. "Just make a 'U' with one foot, then the other, back and forth." Trembling in front of thirty-two other students (every classroom was crammed to capacity then), I stiffly moved my skinny legs back and forth, back and forth, lip-syncing with the microphone as the record went around and around on the record player. I thought I would die.

As revenge to Miss Peterson, Scott (the same one who put me up to that icicle mischief, and later, Charlie's best man), caused a grand commotion in the middle of a filmstrip one afternoon. While the lights were off, he managed to insert the silver-coated paper from chewing gum into the electric outlet, which produced a mighty *sizzle-snap-pop*! and a spray of sparks. The classroom burst into frenzy. Miss Peterson flipped on the room lights! There, lying on his back, looking absolutely dead, was Scott, who, after several seconds of appropriate audience horror, sat up and brushed his hair back with the palm of his hand. Miss Peterson must have put her two-week notice in that same day, because she left before our school year was over.

Did I mention I was skinny? I was so skinny I'd make a chocolate shake every night and add two raw eggs (that was before anyone worried about food poisoning from raw eggs). I was so skinny my Grandpa Pete would tell me, "Mary, if a wind comes along, it'll blow you away just like a kite!" Then he'd proceed to eat the fat from freshly grilled steaks and tell me that all that gristle was good for a person. I was so skinny that I'd wear fuzzy white tights during the school year to make my legs appear bigger.

My report cards usually said, "Mary's a good student, but she doesn't live up to her full potential." This doesn't surprise me now. Though I enjoyed learning, most of the time I was bored. And though I managed to get As and Bs, I never felt an inner motivation to be at the top of my class. I was interested in respectable grades, and somehow I knew that getting Cs was below my ability level. I dabbled at art and enjoyed painting a sixth grade classroom mural, but when art teachers would say, "Oh, you're a Gazelka! I had your sisters Sherry and Susan a few years back. Now they're very talented artists!" that was enough for me to quit. When I took an interest in track and jumping hurdles, a gym teacher said, "Oh, you're a Gazelka! I heard your brother Mark just set a new track record at the high school!" I knew I wasn't zealous enough to compete with my artistic sisters or my athletic older brother. So instead, I found my interests outside of school. And from my weeklong stints at Camp Ojiketa, I knew what I really wanted. A horse.

With persistence (which meant that I hounded my parents day and night about getting what I wanted until in a moment of fatigue they said, "Well, maybe" or "Hmmm, we'll see," at which point I knew I was home free!), I got a horse. Or rather, my sister Susan and I got a horse, but really, deep down, it was my horse, and we named her Watonka. I'm ashamed to say how unprepared my family and I were to bring a horse to our three acres. One Sunday, my sister and I spotted an ad in the St. Paul paper. My dad said, "Well, we'll just drive down and see…," which we knew in our heart of hearts meant we were getting a horse. We arrived at a little farm and looked at the tawny Arab-Welch pony with a brown dorsal stripe down her back.

"She hasn't been ridden in some time," the white-haired man said.

"That doesn't matter," my sister said.

"We love her!" I added.

"So," the farmer said to my dad, "'S'pose you'll wanna come back with your horse trailer tomorrow."

"Oh, no," my dad (a businessman with little mechanical sense) replied. "We'll just cross-tie her in our flatbed trailer."

To my horror now, I remember the whites of her eyes showing as she stood roped from her halter to four-points on our flatbed trailer with foot-high wooden walls as we whisked down the Twin Cities freeways back to our suburban hobby farm. Within the week, I was tapping dirt around fence posts dropped into fresh holes in our field. My dad made plans to build a two-stall horse shelter, which he did—probably the proudest accomplishment of all his projects over the years. And I soon discovered enough courage to ride on my own.

By horseback, I traveled well beyond our long gravel driveway to explore fields filled with goldenrod and yarrow, to discover trails that wound through woods of oaks and maples, to make friends with other horse owners of my age, to find adventure on my own. How could this world away from school—where I found freedom and my horse's complete acceptance of me the way I was—how could this experience compare with going to school and having to stare down my own insecurities? At school, with its crowded halls and constant chatter and buzzing schedule, I struggled with my identity and felt I never measured up, was never enough. On the bare back of my horse, for I usually rode bareback, I was comfortable in my own skin. I knew who I was.

No wonder, then, that my books do not revolve around school settings. School was not the place I felt alive. Rather, I tended to feel my real self was "on hold" until I was out of school.

If I were in school today, most likely I would be diagnosed as having ADD. I struggled to pay attention to directions. I struggled when reading through directions, and still do. I'm embarrassed to say how many times I have to read cookbook directions over and over and over. My mind is easily distracted even now as an adult. School was filled with distractions, and perhaps that's partly why it was hard for me to become passionate about my studies. I always felt I was bouncing along, hoping to stay on top of things, but never really engaging with any single subject or activity in a meaningful way. Being outside and in nature always focuses me. Being physical focuses my mind, and though getting involved in a sport might have been beneficial for me in those school years, sports for girls was a relatively new concept. Volleyball, swimming, and track were options. But when it came right down to it, I preferred a less structured after-school life. That's why having a horse was, for me, a saving grace during the end of my "wandering years."

One of my girlfriends, Corrine, suggested I go to an outdoor rock concert with her when I was in ninth grade. My parents, when I asked them, gave me a clear, one-word answer: "No." But Corrine was fun and cool, and I knew she knew more than I did about life. When my parents were away on a trip and my grandparents were filling in, I took a chance—and went with her to the concert. I was beside myself with daring, wondering what was around the corner as we stepped out of her mother's car and we were left standing there. Amplified music blared over the walls of the old baseball stadium. We found our way in through the crowd and to my first rock concert. I was excited and buzzing with enthusiasm. Beer flowed from kegs, and sweet-smelling smoke rose in swirls from every other concert-goer. "That's pot," Corrine said. "Can you smell it?" It wasn't like anything I'd smelled before. The day was hot, thick with the smells of sweating bodies, popcorn, spilled beer, and marijuana. A swaggering man bumped into me and spilled beer across my chest. A fistfight broke out beside one couple lying on a blanket. People shouted, chanted, sang at the top of their lungs. As the day wore on and the sun baked my brains and my ears ached with too much noise, I wanted to go home. Part of me felt defiant, that as a fourteen-year-old, I had crossed an important bridge into adulthood. But another part of me, the part that was truly *me*, knew that I didn't fit in with this scene. I didn't want to fit in. Shortly after I arrived home, when my parents found out about my going to the rock concert against their orders, I was grounded for three weeks. But I really didn't mind. Summer wasn't yet over. I knew that Corrine and I were not destined to be best friends. And I still had the lake and my horse.

By my senior year, I had been nominated for Homecoming Queen and Snowball Queen—and though it was fun and flattering, at a deeper level, I didn't care (and bowed out of the Snowball nomination, as I'd found a way to graduate early).

High school years were relatively good years for me. To support my new horse, an Appaloosa named Keema, I worked part-time jobs outside of school. I served up malts, sundaes, and burgers at Bridgman's, my first job. I clerked at Rosedale at several clothing stores, and when I was asked to model clothes by my employer for the local fashion show, I reluctantly agreed, especially since my greatest fear was of anything onstage.

When I discovered that I could make more working for maintenance, I did, and instead washed and waxed shopping mall floors with a giant machine that threatened to run away with me. I broke ground as their first female employee and felt good about that.

Modeling clothes at a local fashion show in high school. Credit: From archives of Mary Casanova. Reprinted with permission.

When I had free time, I rode Keema. I also went downhill skiing, sailing, and camping along Lake Superior with friends. My high school circle of friends included individuals who were interested in living well, following their dreams, discussing ideas—and having fun without drugs and alcohol.

A few high school teachers stretched my mind, abilities, and love for learning. One was a political science teacher who expected logical essays, another was a teacher of Russian history whose flaming red hair matched his dramatic style of bringing Russian history, with all its czars and communists, regal splendor and bloody revolutions to life (and history, I realized for the first time, comes alive when it's told as stories). One English teacher taught a course called College Preparatory Writing and gave me the keys to understanding essay form and structure, which certainly helped me write my way through college classes; and finally, there was my dear and favorite English teacher, Mrs. Eunice Jensen.

Eunice Jensen taught a course called "The Bible as Literature." Though I don't remember much about the course, I do remember spending moments after class and after school discussing life, ideas, and books with her. She introduced me to *The Little Prince*, *The Giving Tree*, and other lighthearted and poignant stories. Sometimes I'd miss the last bus (I'd like to say I have overcome being late, but I'm still working on that) and she would say, "No problem, Mary. I can give you a ride home … you're right on my way." And on the way, we'd stop at Dairy Queen, where Mrs. Jensen introduced me to raspberry sundaes. Nothing has ever tasted sweeter, and I'm sure it's because, coming from a family where I felt I never had time alone with my own parents, where I often felt lost in the numbers, here was someone who saw me, heard me, and valued what I had to say.

A few years ago, wanting very much to thank Mrs. Jensen for making a difference in my life, I called my old high school, but they didn't have any contact information, as she hadn't been teaching there for some time. About that same time, I spoke at a literature conference open to the public. I showed my high school photo along with the rest of my PowerPoint program. After I was done speaking, a soft-eyed woman with laugh lines came up to me and said, "You're *my* Mary!" I looked at her and recognized her immediately. "And you're *my* Mrs. Jensen!" She expressed how proud she was of me and that she had no idea that I had become a published author. Of course, how would she? Changing my name from Gazelka to Casanova

Senior photo from Mounds View High School, St. Paul, Minnesota. Credit: From the archives of Mary Casanova. Reprinted with permission.

would throw many people off track. I had the chance to thank her for making a difference, and I meant it from the bottom of my heart.

"You know," she said, "I had another student who went on to illustrate a children's book. She won a big award, the—the..."

"The Caldecott?" I asked.

"Yes, that was it!" Eunice's blue eyes sparkled with the same delight I'd seen years before. "Peggy Rathmann. She wrote a story about a policeman and his dog, I believe."

"Oh! *Officer Buckle and Gloria*! I love that book."

Who would have guessed that unassuming Mrs. Jensen would have produced two children's authors? She reminded me in that moment that we can never know the ripple effect of our lives and how we might touch others. She was a teacher who made a difference because she took the time to see her students as individuals. She took the time to show that she truly cared. Would I have become an author without Mrs. Jensen's influence on my life? Maybe. Maybe not. All I know is that she made a difference and I'm very, very grateful.

Midway through my senior year I found a loophole in the graduation requirements. For students who had jobs outside of school, an extra credit or two could be applied toward overall credits, giving me—and four other girls whom I talked into my idea—the chance to graduate in January, pack our bikes, and take them with us via Greyhound to Bonita Springs, Florida, where we spent a month on the beach in an unfurnished condo. We slept in sleeping bags on the floor, strolled the beach by day, and rode our bikes in the cooler hours of evening.

I returned home, worked to save more money, and that summer bought my Grandpa Pete's rusty blue station wagon for $25 and drove with my friend Mary Haub to Aspen, Colorado. The vehicle smoked blue-black as we climbed the mountain pass, but somehow we made it. Within a day, we landed jobs as maids with accompanying lodging. I was off on another adventure.

My year as a ski bum in Colorado was a year of biking in the fall to Maroon Bells, towering peaks that look over a little lake surrounded by aspen trees that shimmer like real gold; skiing every day that I had free in the winter with my Season Pass strapped around my neck; playing the piano at "après ski" at a lodge; doing maid work for Ethel Kennedy and her family and finding how real this family was, despite their burden of name recognition; and making friends of all ages from across the globe who came and went from that ski town. A Minnesotan, however, isn't used to sunny blue skies every day and having a steady diet of fine weather. Before long, I actually missed the moody climate of the Midwest with its frequent gloomy patches of gray—those rainy days when you turn inward and read a good book. In the Rockies, precipitation seemed to fall mostly at night. Days consisted of clear blue skies. I was out of rhythm. I couldn't "play" all day, every day. After a year I was ready to go to college and back to Minnesota.

College for me was almost synonymous with getting married. After a year of college, I reconnected with Charlie Casanova, who wandered in off the street one day into Hoigaard's, a ski shop where I worked in Dinkytown, the funky area near the University of Minnesota. We shared a love of "going up north" on the weekends to wilder parts of Minnesota, and we loved discussing politics, values, and ideas late into the night. We didn't want to live together, yet we couldn't be apart from one another, so we got married and worked our way through college, graduating together in 1981 from the University of Minnesota's Duluth campus.

I considered several majors in college: art, because I loved throwing pots on the wheel; history, because I loved European and Russian history classes with their richly textured stories; journalism, because I thought that might be an employable path for a writer; and English, because it placed an emphasis on creative writing. I finally settled on a B.A. in English, not for practical reasons, but because it was my heart's

Married at twenty-one in Stillwater, Minnesota, Mary and Charlie walk down the aisle, July 1, 1978. Credit: From the archives of Mary Casanova. Reprinted with permission.

desire to pursue writing, even though I had no idea what kind of writer I wanted to be. I loved Tolstoy's and Dostoevsky's moral undertones and Hemingway's clear, concise language. I loved shaping images into words and experiences into vignettes. I mentored students in writing and helped college friends edit their essays. I did an internship at the local public television station and wrote news releases and ad copy. Anything related to writing felt like the closest fit with my natural abilities and dreams, even if I was still bewildered about what my actual writing niche might someday be.

In Duluth, one English professor, Ray Smith, encouraged me to keep writing. "You could be a freelance writer," he said one day in his office as he handed a paper back to me. "You're good. I believe you have what it takes." Though I honestly couldn't imagine what he saw worth encouraging in my writing at that time, I held onto his words tightly. As a published poet, he focused his classes on sensory detail, meter, and the use of figurative language. It was the only writing class that I recall that helped me better understand the craft of writing. My college education gave me the basics and a broad overview of subject areas, but I never felt truly stretched, truly challenged, even though I maintained a 4.0 GPA in my last two years at college (while working twenty to thirty hours a week). Still, I'm glad that I had a chance to get the education I had and a college degree.

At twenty-five years old, Charlie and I tossed our graduation caps skyward and decided we wanted to follow our dream of living "up north" and away from a metropolitan area. "Why drive to the wilderness on weekends" we reasoned, "if we can find a way to live there year round and drive on occasion to the Twin Cities instead?" Our friends thought we were crazy, but the day we left college we said yes to a business opportunity in International Falls, a remote border town perched on the northern edge of Minnesota and Canadian wilderness.

My real education in life—and as a writer—was about to begin.

Becoming a Writer

"Charles Bradley Casanova," announced the graduation speaker. My husband, dressed in cap and gown, rose from his metal chair beside me.

The speaker announced the next name on the list. "Mary Jean Casanova." I joined Charlie in the aisle, and hand in hand, we proceeded to the stage, symbolically fitting since we'd worked our way through college together as poor married students. One of our apartments was so small that the kitchen sink was within arm's reach of our bed. Our budget was so tight that we wrote grocery menus: oatmeal for breakfast, peanut butter-and-jelly sandwiches for lunch, and mackerel loaf (made from canned mackerel, which was cheaper than tuna fish), spaghetti, or liver and onions (because liver was by far the cheapest meat available) for dinner. Though we were poor, we cooked together, ate our dinners by candlelight, and dined using cloth napkins, making use of wedding gifts.

We shared a desire to live further north, closer to wilderness, and to be independently employed. So when an opportunity presented to take over an insurance agency on the Minnesota-Canada border, we didn't pass it up. We agreed to move to International Falls, three hours north of the University of Minnesota's Duluth campus. Though I knew little about life in a remote, small town, my main career goal was to write, which I could do anywhere. It was only one of many risks we would take to create the life we wanted.

International Falls is smack-dab on the northern border of Minnesota and is not generally considered a Mecca for artists and writers. As I became acquainted with the town's most prominent features—a paper mill, a paper product plant, and a large statue of Smokey Bear in the city park—I wondered how I would survive as a writer. Well, if the adage is true that "Life is what you make it," then nowhere is that more true than in a town where temperatures can dip to sixty below, where the nearest city of any size is hours away, and where small-town ways are firmly entrenched due to its isolation. It's a town where everyone knows everyone, even newcomers. Growing up in the outskirts of St. Paul, I was far more comfortable being unknown, and I didn't much relish the feeling that everyone knew everyone's business.

In our first year there, we bought a mobile home on the edge of fields and woods, where we hiked and cross-country skied. In the extra bedroom, I set up my own writing desk and book shelves. I thought then that if I didn't take my own writing seriously, no one else would either. And so, with the title from Virginia Woolf in mind, I needed "a room of one's own." In my writing space, I journaled. I wrote about what I might want to write about someday. I tried writing short stories, poetry, and articles, and never sent them anywhere. I devoured writing magazines from the public library, such as *The Writer* and *Writers' Digest*, and read everything I could get my hands on about writing. I began collecting a shelf of my favorite books on writing, include the elegantly simple classic by E.B. White, *The Elements of Style*.

Within a year, however, my steam for writing shifted. We were expecting our first child. On November 8, 1982, Kate was born, and

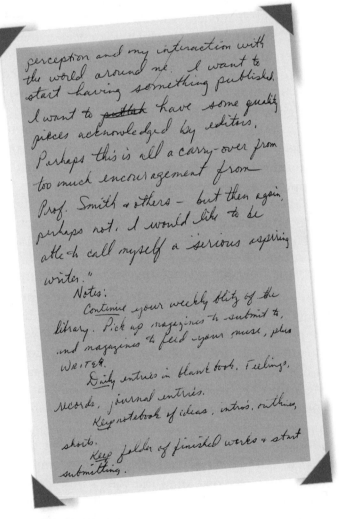

A journal entry in 1981, shortly after college. Credit: From the archives of Mary Casanova. Reprinted with permission.

before we brought her home from the Falls Memorial Hospital, my writing corner turned into a diaper changing table. Totally in love with Kate and passionate about being a good mother, I left my writing simmering on the rear burner. I still journaled—amidst days that seemed to spill into one another with cleaning, with feedings, with diaper changing, with laundry, with cooking—and as I wrote my inner world down, page by page, my own words helped me keep in touch with myself. Journaling kept me limber as a writer and helped keep my writing dream alive, and my entries frequently ended in prayers.

When Kate was one, we moved to a little home beside Ranier Beach. Having grown up on water, I knew this could be a wonderful place to raise our children: no matter that in the dead of winter frost lined the house's uninsulated walls and we were forced to close off the bedrooms and sleep in the living room to keep warm; no matter that in the spring, water flowed like a river over the rock foundation of our basement. Once when my dad visited, he joked, "Well, you two, if

Launching a family, business, and writing dream wasn't easy. Credit: From the archives of Mary Casanova. Reprinted with permission.

times get tough you could open up a trout fishing business in your basement!"

Times were tough. About the time Charlie assumed his insurance agency, one of the paper plants closed down, and hundreds of workers were let go. He lost business faster than he could add it. We lived barely from paycheck to paycheck, and though I began to write résumés for people, I chose to be financially tight over working full time and putting Kate in day care.

To keep at my writing dream, I enrolled in a freelance writing correspondence course through a program in Colorado. The weekly and monthly assignments helped me to shape characters and story settings, and to think about the marketplace. I wrote a short story for a publication called *Loonfeather*, a small regional literary journal. To my amazement and delight, they bought my story. If I was paid anything, and I don't remember now, it wasn't much. It didn't matter. I was thrilled to be published and to see my words in print. And I was hooked.

Our son, Eric, made his way into our lives on December 8, 1985. I thought having a second child would be easier and would give me more time to write. Any mother knows that couldn't be further from the truth.

"Mom!" Kate would shout, exasperated. "Tell him to stop crying!"

Eric was as easy a baby as any parent could hope for. But every baby has to cry once in a while. Kate took matters into her own hands—or teeth. When Eric was old enough to stand in his crib in the room they shared, she nipped his toes to quiet him down. That was the night we started looking for a three-bedroom house.

When I circled the barn-style turn-of-the-century house on Rainy Lake, I said out loud, "I could grow old here." Seagulls circled overhead, a train whistled and rumbled over the trestle bridge that joined the United States with Canada, and the house sat on a bay where the lake and river converged: a home that any writer would love. Little did I know then that a whole series of books (*Dog Watch*) and a historic novel (*The Red Skirt's Girl*) would be set in that location. In 1986, the housing market was deflated and the price of the lake home within our reach. We stretched our finances and bought it.

When Kate and Eric were preschoolers, I devoted myself to baking cookies, doing crafts, reading stories, pushing swings, taking hikes, and playing lifeguard. We decided to go without television for the first eight years of parenting, and instead emphasized the outdoors, reading, and music, including piano and cello lessons.

Realizing that I wasn't finding my niche as a writer, I turned to teaching writing and began filling in at Rainy River Community College as adjunct faculty while I started a master's degree in English at Bemidji State University, a two-hour drive from home. I taught a workshop in business writing through community education. I filled in at the college and taught freshman composition, creative thinking, study skills, and speed reading (which strikes me as funny since I still think of myself as a reader who savors words and moves slowly through text). After teaching eight classes in 1988–89, I looked forward to taking a two-credit workshop at the Split Rock Arts Program at UMD (the University of Minnesota, Duluth campus). The course that caught my eye was taught by Marion Dane Bauer, and it was "Writing for Children," a two-credit, weeklong workshop. Since I had always loved writing, this seemed an appealing course to add to my graduate work.

Marion gave me the keys to my life that week. First, she opened the doors to a field I had never considered. Suddenly, authors I had never known as a kid were speaking to me: Gary Paulsen, Natalie Babbitt, Katherine Paterson.... It's a cliché, forgive me, but the light bulb really did turn on in my brain. I knew with clarity that this was the genre for me. I loved the challenge of writing sparely, of writing clearly, of writing from a child's heart.

Marion Dane Bauer is a fine teacher. Though I had taken various writing courses in college, I had never quite grasped how to take what I felt emotionally and transfer my inner world to a fictitious character. Up until that point as a writer, I'd often said, "Oh, I write vignettes." I wrote slices of real life that never quite reached the level of story. Marion emphasized the need to stay inside a character's viewpoint, to ask, "What does your character want?" And knowing what the character wants is critical, because it gives a character motivation. Conflict rises up to confound the character's deepest yearnings and increases the stakes for the character. (I highly recommend Marion's book *What's Your Story?* for a more in-depth look at crafting stories through Marion's words.)

The first novel I started (and never finished) was about a girl who has lost her mother to cancer. Her father was emotionally distant, lost in his own grief, and my character needed to journey through her own grief by taking action. She runs away from home in the opening chapter. Though I wasn't able to finish that novel, it was the first time I was able to sink inside a character and feel her emotions. I understood loss: my mother-in-law, Rita Casanova, had died just a few years earlier from cancer. And now, looking back, I see myself more clearly in the character: running away. But in real life I didn't have to run away. I was able to begin processing my own struggles, my own emotions, my own loss— through my fictitious character.

By the end of that weeklong workshop, I was passionate about writing for children. Would I ever get published? Did I have a chance at becoming an author? I had no way of knowing. My work in the class didn't blow Marion away, as I recall. What mattered more to me at that point was that I finally knew what I wanted to pursue. I had direction, a sense of purpose—a passion—and that was by itself a gift.

Later, when another professor and I were discussing my long-range goals at the community college, she asked, "But Mary, which do you really want to do more? Teach or write?"

"Write," I said, and decided to forego finishing my master's and instead put my energy more fully into writing. I was thirty-two years old.

Another benefit that came out of Marion's workshop was the awareness that I needed a writers' group to move forward. Marion remarked that one of the other workshop attendees, Lois Berg, who lived in Pengilly, Minnesota, wrote at a similar level. She said, "Even two people meeting can be a writers' group." With her suggestion, Lois and I decided to meet every month. Throughout the year, and despite the conditions—rain, snow, sleet—we drove an hour to meet halfway at a café in Orr, Minnesota. The waitress began to know us by name and ask what we were working on. We critiqued each other's stories and novels, drank volumes of coffee, and, though we were both green, shared a determination to stay open to feedback and to improve our craft as writers.

With young children, I increasingly needed backup for times when I would meet with Lois and when I wanted to attend a writing workshop. Two elderly women, Ione and Dorothy, came into our lives as adopted grandmothers. They doted on Kate and Eric, providing a grandmotherly presence my kids often lacked, and taught them everything from Scrabble to knitting.

One of the leads I followed up on in Marion's class was to do "work for hire," or to write for packagers. She acknowledged that the pay wasn't great, and that you wouldn't get royalties, but it was a way to get published while you were working on breaking into the larger marketplace. She mentioned a packager that was based in Minneapolis at the time named Crestwood House. Determined not to let a crumb pass me by, I sent them my résumé, letting them know I would be interested in writing on any number of topics, from animals to history. After a few phone calls of hounding them for work, my phone rang one day.

"Mary, I think we have a project for you."

"You do?" Panic began to coil in my gut.

"Yes, we're starting a series called 'Top Dog' for Macmillan. We thought you might want to write about one of the breeds."

My heart spiked with adrenalin. Was this what I really wanted? Could I do it? What if I failed miserably? "Thank you! I'd love to. Tell me more."

"The deadline is pretty tight. You have one week to provide us with an outline and then one month to turn in your final draft."

All-out panic. This was crazy! I'd never written anything under a deadline before other than college assignments. This would be a published book? I should back out. Save face. "Okay," I said.

"So what breed of dog would you like to write about?" She read a list of breeds that the series would cover. When she said "golden retriever," I said, "We have one of those. I'll write that one."

"Grandma" Ione filled in for the next month as I turned first to research books from the library and interlibrary loan, made up an outline, began writing note cards and tossing them in stacks around me, and finally began to write a draft on my word processor. (I started with a manual typewriter in college, upgraded to an electric typewriter with word processing capabilities, which I used for *Top Dog*, and changed computers and laptops as technology evolved.)

In less than a year, the manuscript was turned into a skinny hardcover book—but it was indeed a book. By taking on the project, I realized that I loved the process from start to finish, and getting paid $1,000 to write that book was well worth the work. My local newspaper featured me, our own golden retriever, Princess, and my book on the front page of *The Daily Journal*. Suddenly, I was, in the eyes of my small town, a children's author. I enjoyed having a book, but my vision of becoming a writer meant writing fiction, which I turned to again.

About that time, Kate was eight and Eric was five, and I decided to get a horse again in my life. Her name was Lady, or Lady Grey, as she was dappled cloudy gray from muzzle to rump. I had visions of riding as I had when I was younger with my Appaloosa, Keema. But within six months, I knew that the timing of getting this horse was all wrong and decided to sell her. I was heartsick when the buyers drove up in their shiny truck, hopped out and opened up the doors to their horse trailer, and loaded Lady inside. The transaction went smoothly. They wrote me a check, drove off, and I went home and cried. I took my emotions, however, and wrote a short story called "Horse for Sale," about a boy named Elliot who decides it's time to sell his horse, but struggles with his decision after the new owners haul his horse away. By story's end, however, Elliot changes his mind and buys his horse back again. By writing the story, I had processed my own feelings and felt much, much better. I shared the story with my husband.

"Does this mean," Charlie asked, a puzzled expression on his face, "that you're going to buy your horse back again?"

I laughed. "No, honey. As a writer, I can give emotions and struggles to my characters that I might identify with, but I can change the endings from what happens in real life."

"Oh. I see."

He really should write his own book on coming to understand living with a writer.

That short story sold to *Cricket* magazine, and I felt I had made a huge breakthrough as a writer. I began to understand how to truly step inside my characters and allow them to be different than me, yet share genuine emotions with my main characters.

Similarly, around that time period, I wrote another short story, drawing from something that troubled me in real life. One of Charlie's secretaries who was my age suddenly lost her husband to a heart attack. Left behind were two sons, boys that I knew. My heart went out to them. How would I feel if I was in their shoes? When I heard about them having to gather their father's clothing and boots from the hospital, a vivid image of worn leather boots filled my mind. I sat down and wrote about what might happen when two orphaned boys go camping and one insists on wearing his father's oversized boots and titled my short story "Father's Boots."

On a lark, I submitted the story to a writing contest at the annual Children's Literature Conference in Grand Forks, North Dakota. Jean Craighead George spoke at that first conference, along with Lisa Westberg Peters, and I attended with my friend Lois Berg. To my astonishment, at the end of the conference, they announced the winner of the Emily Award. My short story had won! Fluttering with nervousness, I made the long trek down the small auditorium aisle to accept the medal, which they put around my neck. I had never in my life won a single medal, blue ribbon, or top award for anything. Never. Imagine my astonishment. That a committee of authors had seen publishing promise in my short work of fiction was reward enough to last me a long, long time. To top that off, however, they handed me an unexpected check for $250.

I went home with the Emily Award medallion around my neck. My husband and children were proud, but I was prouder. It was the first time I started to believe I might have potential as a published author. I wanted to push myself hard enough to find out what I could accomplish. No one had ever had any real expectations of me, and I had never had high expectations for myself. Suddenly, I wanted to see what I could accomplish—if I applied myself. What if I lived up to my full potential? I began to write picture books, short stories, and novels for children.

The following summer, I went to a workshop at Chautauqua in upstate New York. The weeklong workshop is sponsored annually by *Highlights for Children*, the magazine I fondly remember combing through in the waiting room of my childhood dentist's office. Going to Chautauqua meant a big investment, and I wasn't sure that I could come up with over $2,000 for the conference and travel expenses, especially since I wasn't making any real money as a writer at that time. But I have learned over and over to listen to my gut, and I *knew* that if I was going to progress to the next level as a writer, the timing of attending Chautauqua was *now*. I sought out state and local grants that supported writers, jumped through paperwork hoops and submitted writing samples and my proposed plan of attending this conference, and crossed my fingers. If I couldn't get financial help, I would have to simply let the idea go. To my gratitude and amazement, however, I received funding from the Minnesota State Arts Board and their regional arm, the Arrowhead Regional Arts Council. With both funding sources, I was able to swing going to the conference, and it made all the difference.

Aspiring writers need to be creative in keeping their dream alive. To work alone, in a complete vacuum, without the support of other writers or meeting authors and editors, can become discouraging. Many writers I have met along the way have quit after sending out one manuscript and receiving their first rejection. I think I kept following my passion for writing for children by being in a writers' group (of two at the time), by attending writing conferences to expand my knowledge of the field, and by seeking funding to make attending conferences possible. It took creativity and determination in those early years, but I'm so glad I didn't try to learn the craft completely on my own. I highly doubt I would have a career in this field today if I hadn't invested time and money in learning from other published authors and from editors I met along the way.

Before I left for the Chautauqua conference, I labeled paper lunch bags with days of the week: Monday, Tuesday, etc. Kate and Eric were eight and five years old, and I worried about being apart from them. I wanted to make sure that each day I was gone they could look forward to opening up a bag and finding a note, a few treats, and small toys. While Charlie was at work, "Grandma Ione" or "Grandma Dorothy" came to babysit. I struggled to part from my role as full-time mother, but I knew I needed to expand as a writer.

My eight days at Chautauqua in 1991 changed my sense of what was possible. I mentored with two authors: Dayton O. Hyde, a novelist who lives on a wild mustang reserve in South Dakota, and Pam Conrad, novelist and picture book writer, who became a dear friend and a significant mentor in my life. The days were as tightly packed as pickle jars, with workshops on craft, individualized meetings with mentors, shoptalk at meal time, and sitting through afternoon lectures.

Like a marathon runner pausing at roadside rests, I was thirsty for knowledge and understanding and drank up everything that week. At the time, I brought the first two chapters of *Moose Tracks* for critique. Dayton Hyde helped me understand that I needed to make every word count, and that by writing "The room was heavy with his father's disapproval," I was making strong use of metaphor. He encouraged me to use sensory details, too, and to weave them in page by page.

Pam Conrad, bless her, looked at me and seemed to see my future. She told me, "You're going to make it in this field, Mary. Someday you'll be earning a six-digit income."

"That's nice of you to say," I managed, wondering how she could possibly have that much faith in me based on meeting me and reading only two chapters of my fledgling novel.

We spent many hours walking the grounds of the historic village of Chautauqua and strolling along the lake. She advised me to send my manuscript to a few editors, including Andrea Cascardi, an editor at a relatively new publisher then—Hyperion, a Disney publisher. She knew this editor personally and had worked with her and thought my style might appeal to Andrea. "And go ahead and mention in your cover letter that I suggested sending it to her." (Getting published isn't about who you know, since the manuscript itself must grab an editor's attention, but including Pam's recommendation did mean that my manuscript made it out of the "slush pile" and onto Andrea's desk rather than straight into the hands of a "slush pile reader," often an intern position or entry-level position in publishing. That's why attending conferences and making connections can help shorten the time it takes to get a manuscript through the labyrinth of readers at a publishing house.)

That long week away, I felt my chin begin to lift and I started to see my own potential as others reflected it back to me. In the week's closing comments, Pam said from the podium to everyone that one of her goals was to "keep in touch with Mary Casanova." My friend Lois Berg and newer friends Barb Santucci, Kay Winters, and Candice Fleming (all published authors now) beamed at me. I returned home, buoyant enough to touch the clouds.

I stayed in touch with Pam Conrad through the next few years while she battled breast cancer. She treated me as a peer, though I held her on a high, dazzling pedestal. Shortly after selling *Moose Tracks* to Hyperion, I took on a teaching position with the Institute of Children's Literature in West Redding, Connecticut—you know, the one that advertises in magazines everywhere: "Do you want to write for children?" I flew into New York City and stopped over at Pam's home on Long Island. She put on a small dinner party that included me—to my amazement—my Hyperion editor, Andrea Cascardi; Jim Giblin, author and Clarion editor; and another literary friend whose name I do not recall. I was out of my league, yet Pam didn't see me that way. Maybe she saw herself in me—coming from working roots, making her way independently as a writer—and wanted to give someone else a "leg up." Pam truly modeled the importance of mentorship.

A year or so later, after Pam's cancer had progressed further, I stopped out again when I was on a visit to see editors in New York City. We strolled the boardwalk on Long Island on a windy fall day. The sun radiated off the ocean and beach, and we sat down, side by side in the sand, talking.

"What are you learning now, Pam, in the midst of your cancer?"

She paused, pulled off her blond wig to reveal her bald head, and scratched. "Oh that feels good! You don't know how much a wig itches until you have to wear one." Then she gazed out at the ocean, considering my question. "I think I'm learning how to become more *Pam* every day."

Pam passed away too soon, and I remember feeling lost without her as a guide and mentor, completely on my own as a new author. But I've often remembered her words, especially in light of having to become a more public figure. All I need to do is be more *Mary* every day. That's all any of us can do: to be true to our best selves, our most authentic selves, and risk being who we are—every day.

In my struggle to get published, I developed a record-keeping log of where I sent manuscripts, when they came back, and whether they were rejected or accepted. I made it my goal to gather as many rejections as possible rather than expect quick success. From college to the publication of *Moose Tracks*, I received over two hundred rejection letters of various sorts, and those were all part of the learning process, part of my training in what worked and didn't work. Most importantly, I stayed in process and kept at it. Like a juggler with a dozen balls whirling through the air, I tried to keep several manuscripts circulating at once. Far better to have hope that there were still editors who might accept one of my stories than to receive a rejection on my last circulating manuscript. It was as if I had to guard my emotional self from my practical self: the writer in me kept writing and the marketer in me kept the manuscripts flying out the door. When I started to get handwritten notes in the margins of form letters that said "Not quite right for us, but send us more of your work," I knew I was getting closer.

As I drafted stories, I read them aloud to my children and asked them for feedback. They became my frontline editors, unafraid to tell me if something was boring or unclear, yet rewarding me with their rapt attention when a story was working.

I sent *Moose Tracks* off to publishers and to agents. When two publishers were interested in my novel if I was willing to revise it, I decided I needed an agent to get in the middle of the process. Out of five agents I had in mind, Kendra Marcus (Bookstop Agency, Orinda, California), agreed to represent me. Getting an agent isn't any easier than getting a publisher, but having two publishers interested in my novel certainly had to help. I revised ruthlessly, cutting out characters, changing scenes, rewriting the ending—and then I sent the manuscript back. When the phone rang one afternoon, I was met with the happiest words any writer can hear. "I love your rewrite," Andrea Cascardi said, "and I would like to make you an offer on *Moose Tracks*." I just about dropped the phone. That evening, I went out to dinner with my family and celebrated, thankful to be with my husband and children and to share a landmark moment in my path as a writer.

The Writer

The next few years were a boiling cauldron of activity. My writing career developed in the midst of a busy family life. And though I never fully achieved it, "balance" became the code word of those years. When Jane Kurtz, my friend and an author from Grand Forks, North Dakota, and I compared notes on how we were managing our budding writing careers, our main concern was how to balance our passion for our writing with the needs and responsibilities of family life. We share the belief that finding balance between those worlds is a lifelong process, and some seasons of life make that process more challenging than others. I look back now from the vantage point of having my children at college, and I wonder how I managed to write anything back when Kate and Eric were younger. When something is truly important, however, we manage to find time for it.

After the publication of *Moose Tracks*, we took in our first exchange student, Wu Geng Hui from China (in the following years we would host Evi from Belgium, Christine from France, and Fernando from Brazil). We volunteered for school events, Little League, and Sunday school.

One frigid winter day, our family volunteered to help with the Eslinger sled dog race. We piled hay bales at a particularly sharp corner on the snowy trail, huddled around cups of hot chocolate, and later visited with the mushers at the race's finish. Two Siberian husky pups waited to find new owners. We returned home with two more dogs (we already had a golden retriever and a miniature schnauzer at home) and started our own small team. Eventually, we owned five Siberians, enough to pull the dog sled in winter and a chariot-cart along the dirt roads in the other three seasons.

Activities like this invigorated me, even if it meant adding one more thing to our already full lives. Though I love to write, physical activity and time outdoors renews me. I need both. We spent Saturdays with Kate and Eric on the frozen landscape of Rainy Lake, watching our kids whisk along over the ice with the dogs. With dog harnesses that criss-cross a dog's back, we learned to skijor: the dog pulls, and the cross-country skier is tethered behind with a rope attached to a waist belt. It's quite fast and as thrilling as downhill skiing! One neighbor watched me wipe out three times on my skis with starts that left me facedown on snow before I successfully got underway with two huskies. One husky, I learned the hard way, was much more manageable than two.

In the summer, to better engage with Rainy Lake as a family, we bought and renovated an old forty-eight-foot houseboat. I'd often bring along my laptop and plug it into an inverter, which drew power from the boat's batteries so that I could continue working on whatever writing project was underway. We started spending so much time on the houseboat that we purchased a lot on Jackfish Island so we could tie up at our own dock for long weekends. One weekend, my friend, children's author John Coy, and his daughter, Sophie, came up to visit. Both John and I had published at least one book, and we were fledgling authors eager to talk about writing. He and his daughter met my family at the marina after sunset, with darkness falling. We used a spotlight to help navigate our way to Jackfish Island. Rainy Lake is a vast wilderness lake dotted with endless bays, inlets, and islands. It's easy to get lost, especially at night, and it's all too easy to hit rocks—big rocks— as they're everywhere. It's a lake that requires knowledge and a map. When we arrived at our dock on Jackfish Island, it was pitch dark. Kate, Eric, and Sophie hopped off the houseboat. "Ew! Something stinks!"

John and Charlie started to scout around for the source of the offending odor. "Must be a carp that floated up on shore," Charlie said. But what they found brought sheer puzzlement.

"What is it?" I joined the kids and clustered close to the awful-smelling object. Lights from our flashlights revealed something big, something alien, something that looked like a large animal body with fleshy human palms. My creative imagination soared. "What is it? From another planet?"

"It's creepy!" said Kate.

Finally, ever the rock of wisdom and steadiness, Charlie gave the verdict. "It's a bear, only it's probably been in the water so long it has lost most of its hair."

Boy, was I relieved.

To move the carcass away from the boat and out into the bay, Charlie used the gaff hook, which punctured the body enough to let out a loud "whoosh" and a smell more dreadful than—well, more dreadful than a badly decomposing bear. Real men, John and Charlie took turns pushing it "out to sea," or at least into the moving water of Rainy Lake, which flowed into Rainy River.

Someday, maybe I'll use that event in a story, one memorable time when my writing life and family life overlapped.

Kate and Eric were involved in karate, music, horseback lessons, church activities, downhill skiing, snowboarding, skating, swimming, cross-country, football, rollerblading, biking, waterskiing, and wakeboarding. We ate home-cooked dinners together every evening, and our kids and exchange students shared in household chores.

In the middle of these years, I taught writing workshops at the community college, wrote new novels and picture books (*Riot, Wolf Shadows*, and *The Hunter*), and taught for the Institute of Children's Literature (ICL). The Institute is located in West Redding, Connecticut, and to teach for them I went to the old multi-roomed mansion for training. I laugh now at my grand entrance. I had been instructed to take the Connecticut Limo service from New York City. I visited editors first in New York, headed to Long Island to visit Pam Conrad, and then tried to call the Connecticut Limo service. I couldn't seem to find their listing in the phone book. So, I did the next best thing and called Airport Limo, and asked them to pick me up on Long Island, which they did—in a shiny black sedan with lovely leather seats. The driver, unlike the yellow cab drivers of New York, wore a black suit and tie. "Where to?" he asked.

"West Redding, Connecticut," I said, and climbed into the backseat, wearing my best jeans and blazer. Not sure what to do on the two-hour trip, I flipped open my laptop to match the part of an author. But I wasn't able to concentrate. Instead, I stared out the window at hills and pine trees passing by. Minnesotans believe they are the only ones with pine trees and most of us, before visiting the East Coast, think it's all pavement from New York City to Boston. I was enchanted to arrive at the Institute, nestled at the end of winding tree-graced roads.

When I submitted my limo bill, the folks at ICL were aghast. After I finished my training period and climbed aboard Connecticut Limo to head back to New York City and LaGuardia Airport, I understood my mistake. The limo was a large van that carried about *sixteen* passengers and their luggage. I felt embarrassed and stupid. Being an author doesn't mean *real* limo service everywhere. Only sometimes.

As I said earlier, I had always been afraid of speaking in front of people. Coming from a big family, it's as if I spent my whole life wanting the spotlight—wanting to be seen and to be heard—until the light actually swung my way. When it did, I wanted to run and hide and be anonymous.

Getting published gradually changed all that; being an author brings with it responsibility. If I care about my books, then I owe it to my work to get out and speak when asked. And with the publication of *Moose Tracks*, requests started coming in.

On my very first reading at The Loft Literary Center in Minneapolis, I understood the meaning of dry mouth. There I was, ready to say hello to the audience, which consisted largely of writing friends, and my tongue stuck to the roof of my mouth. I eyed the glass of water beside the podium. Hands trembling, I brought the glass to my mouth and sipped. Still dry. I sipped again, praying I wouldn't drop the glass, and then began.

With my earliest speaking engagements, I'd toss and turn in bed for months prior to speaking. I had to somehow overcome my fear of speaking, or I'd get ulcers before I turned forty. The only way to get over trembling, stomach-twisting, and dry-mouth was to practice. I was now an author so I figured I'd better learn to stand in the spotlight. I listened to a set of tapes (three times) called "Never Be Nervous Again." I joined Toastmasters, a civic club dedicated to taking the "um's" and "er's" out of speaking, as well as the stomach-turning panic. Toastmasters, though I didn't complete the full menu of courses, helped. And speaking, willing myself to step to the podium, ignoring my own physical meltdowns, helped. Now, years later, I actually enjoy speaking.

That's the thing about writing. There's so much learning along the way! I've learned to pay attention to the world around me for story material. I've learned to hone my listening skills—the ability to listen to that "still, small voice" within that guides us each uniquely. (I do believe that everyone has stories to write and that each of us has stories that only each of us can write. My job is to listen for my own stories and tell them the best that I can.)

Besides learning to speak, I've learned how to pack, to travel, and to carry myself in most social settings. I've been learning about how to be more myself every day, or, in Pam Conrad's words, *more Mary every day.*

And I've made blunders, too, of course. Like the bookseller that I met at a conference who looked glowingly, beautifully pregnant. Her eyes shined; her face was flushed a rosy pink; and her jumper hugged her belly. I smiled, sharing that *knowing* of motherhood that only mothers can truly share. "When are you expecting?" I asked.

"I'm not," she said, maintaining the smile on her face. "I'm just fat."

I wanted the earth to open up and accept me and my humble apologies.

And guess what happened the next year at the same conference? In the whirl of so many people, so many quick conversations, I bumped into her again and out of my mouth came the same bumbling question. "When are you expecting?"

"I'm not," she said, again for the second time to the same bumbling, insensitive, what-are-you-stupid? author. "I'm just fat."

To her credit, and to my astonishment, she still asked me to sign several years in a row at her bookstore. I must have fallen over myself with apologies. Oh, well. Learning is often painful, but I try—I really do try now to not ask that question unless a person is going into labor. Even then, I think I should hold my tongue, just in case I'm wrong.

I would never have so many books published without the help of other writers and authors. Because writing is a solitary craft filled with discouraging rejections along the way, I found that to keep going I needed the companionship and support of other writers. Lois Berg and I continued to meet in Orr, Minnesota, for a few years as a writers' group of two. Eventually, Lois moved to Minneapolis, and I started working with former writing workshop students of mine in International Falls. Out of a "master's" class I taught in children's literature came several talented writers who have become friends and members of my current writing group.

Published authors need writing groups too. Since my local group started meeting, Sheryl Peterson and Shawn Shofner have had several books published. A half dozen in number, we meet at the local coffee shop or at each other's homes. Sometimes we'll go to a cabin for a night or two for a mini-writing retreat, a time of more intense writing and critique. In our critiques, we listen to the writer read from her manuscript, give feedback about what we like, and rather than offer criticism, pose our concerns as questions. The goal is to help each other, but to always respect the author as the creator of her own work. We leave fingerprints on each other's manuscripts, but the work itself belongs wholly to its writer.

Similarly, I belong to another writers' group that meets almost annually on Mallard Island on Rainy Lake. As an emerging author, I had hoped to lure other writers north for a week of relaxation, writing, and group critiques. Lois Berg and I brainstormed for possibilities. Now, nearly fifteen years later, we continue to meet as a group of twelve children's authors and illustrators. Our time is spent canoeing, swimming, cooking together, and reading the many books on the island. I have learned so much from this group of

Writing often begins on Rainy Lake. Mary in 1995 atop her old houseboat. Credit: From the archives of Mary Casanova. Reprinted with permission.

writers. I've started many novels on the island, and the synergy of getting so many creative minds together in a wilderness setting has always helped move me into my work, asking the right questions about a story.

Stories contain conflict, and writing about conflict has been my way of facing issues head-on, which wasn't part of my upbringing. My Scandinavian background likely had much to do with my tendency to stuff my strongest feelings, silence my harshest thoughts, and only cry when I was alone. In short, being "nice" was deemed most important; true honesty that might lead to emotional outbursts was not. If conflict erupted in my family, which was rare, or if anyone raised their voice, I grew quieter and retreated. I learned from my upbringing that if I wanted to get my point across or wanted to get my way, reasoned arguments were the most effective. If I vented or exploded emotionally, which I never—*never*—did, I lost. If I kept up a steady stream of persuasion and maintained "reason," I likely got my way. "Being nice" was an acceptable tool for getting what I wanted in my family; stirring up conflict was not. Coming, then, from that background, no wonder fiction provided me with an outlet for dealing with conflict. Through the myriad of conflicts my characters have faced, I've found more courage in real life to stand my ground, to risk honesty, and to speak up.

The growth in my craft as a writer is intertwined with my growth as a human being. Writing is a catalyst for learning and self-exploration; and the willingness to explore the interior labyrinths of self and soul, no matter how dark and frightening, is a catalyst for writing. I've learned through my writing to be as real and honest as I possibly can.

Our lives have their own chapters. This chapter of my life is good, too. My husband and I often travel together, more recently in a twenty-five-foot motor home (with our dogs). While I speak at schools and conferences across the country, Charlie often handles book sales and is my tour manager. One time when we parked our RV outside a junior high school and walked through the front doors, a teacher told me that her seventh graders had been all abuzz about our arrival, asking, "Is that man her bodyguard?!"

"Well, yes, of sorts, I suppose," she replied. "That's her husband."

Life's road is sweeter when we can travel together, and no matter how well a trip goes, it's always good to return home. Last fall, after returning from a week of speaking, Charlie and I rode our bay horses, side by side down a trail rich with autumn. Aspen wore their finest yellow as our horses trotted along the grassy path. The earth uncorked its cellar's finest, a full-bodied fragrance, not too dry, not too sweet, fermented just so with goldenrod and aster. Overhead, Canada geese honked riotously in an undulating southward V. As we turned our horses toward home, the amber moon rose behind a shim of inky black spruce.

All I could add to the evening was my gratitude.

Nature restores me when I'm world-weary. Nature feeds my creativity. I love being an author and I love creating with words, but my work is an expression of being human, of living in the world of here and now. Writing is also my way of experiencing life twice, of probing experiences and questions more deeply, and of recapturing the sensory world.

On the road, I meet the finest people in the world, from students to educators. Because I value a child as much as an adult, I never talk down to students or underestimate the depth of their intelligence or questions. At my very first school visit, I ended by taking questions and answers. A fifth grade student raised his hand and asked, "What are your long-term aspirations for your writing career?"

I was dumbstruck. Long-term aspirations? I had no idea what I was doing the next day, week, or year. I had published one book and couldn't guess if I would ever be lucky enough to publish another.

"To write," I answered. "One page at a time."

And that's still true. When students ask, "But how do you write a novel?" I answer, "One sentence, one paragraph, one page at a time."

A List of My Books

Cécile: Gates of Gold. Illustrated by Jean-Paul Tibbles. (American Girl/Pleasant Company, 2002).

Cécile has always wished for a royal life, but when she rescues a runaway horse and is rewarded with a place at the palace of Versailles as a servant to Madame's six dogs, Cécile learns that palace life is filled with unforeseen dangers and that she has to be braver than she ever dreamed possible.

Cover art for *Cécile: Gates of Gold* (2002) by Mary Casanova. Cover art by Jean-Paul Tibbles. (American Girl/Pleasant Company). Reprinted with permission.

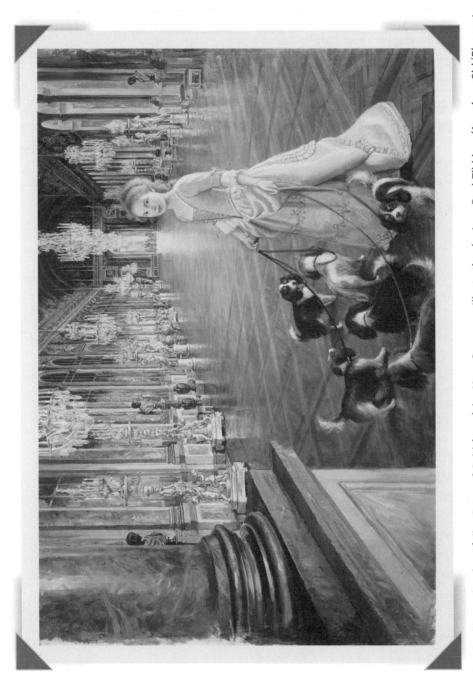

Interior illustration for *Cécile: Gates of Gold* (2002) by Mary Casanova. Illustration by Jean-Paul Tibbles. (American Girl/Pleasant Company). Reprinted with permission.

Curse of a Winter Moon. (Hyperion, 2000).

On her deathbed, Marius's mother requests that he always take care of his younger brother, Jean-Pierre. But Jean-Pierre was born on Christmas Eve, a sign in the 1500s in France that one might be a werewolf, or *loup garou*. In the midst of political and religious upheaval, with superstitions and fears ablaze, Marius's task of watching over his brother becomes increasingly difficult—and dangerous.

Cover art for *Curse of a Winter Moon* (2000) by Mary Casanova. Cover art by Cliff Nielsen. (Hyperion). Reprinted with permission.

Dog Watch, Book 1: *Trouble in Pembrook*. Illustrations by Omar Rayyan. (Aladdin/Simon and Schuster, 2006).

There's trouble brewing in the quiet Minnesota town of Pembrook—the dogs can smell it in the air! So Kito, Chester, and the rest of the gang form Dog Watch, a canine version of Neighborhood Watch. Together they set out to uncover the person (or animal) behind the vandalism in town and to find Tundra, their missing alpha dog.

Reprinted with permission of Aladdin Paperbacks, an imprint of Simon & Schuster Children's Publishing Division. Cover art from *Dog Watch: Trouble in Pembrook* by Mary Casanova, illustrated by Omar Rayyan. Illustrations copyright © 2006 Omar Rayyan.

Dog Watch, Book 2: *Dog-Napped!* Illustrated by Omar Rayyan. (Aladdin/Simon and Schuster, 2006).

Dogs and puppies are disappearing in Pembrook, and Kito and the other dogs of Dog Watch are hot on the trail to find out who is behind the mysterious dog-nappings, before it's too late.

Reprinted with permission of Aladdin Paperbacks, an imprint of Simon & Schuster Children's Publishing Division. Interior illustration from *Dog Watch: Trouble in Pembrook* by Mary Casanova, illustrated by Omar Rayyan. Illustrations copyright © 2006 Omar Rayyan.

Dog Watch, Book 3: *Danger at Snow Hill.* Illustrated by Omar Rayyan. (Aladdin/Simon and Schuster, 2006).

There's trouble again in Pembrook. A mysterious creature—possibly a wolf or a bear—is attacking children on their sleds and getting into garbage at the skating rink's warming house. A villager newcomer thinks the Pembrook dogs are to blame and should stay home—forever! Unless Kito, Chester, and the gang catch the culprit fast, their roaming days are over.

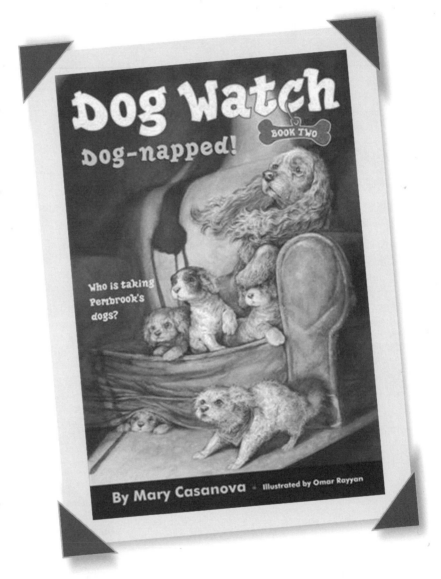

Cover art for Dog Watch, Book 2: *Dog-Napped!* (2006) by Mary Casanova. Cover art by Omar Rayyan. (Aladdin/Simon and Schuster). Reprinted with permission.

The Hunter. Illustrated by Ed Young. (Atheneum, 2000).

A Chinese folktale retold. Hai Li Bu is a good hunter, providing for his villagers as best he can, but when a flood threatens his village, Hai Li Bu must choose between fleeing and saving himself or sacrificing his life to save his village.

Reprinted with the permission of Atheneum Books for Young Readers, an imprint of Simon & Schuster Children's Publishing Division. Cover art from *The Hunter* (2000) by Mary Casanova, illustrated by Ed Young. Illustrations © 2006 Ed Young.

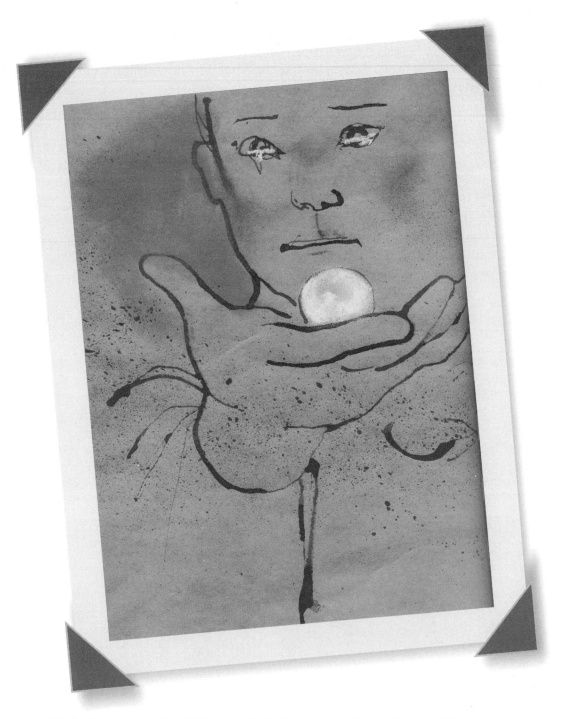

Reprinted with the permission of Atheneum Books for Young Readers, an imprint of Simon & Schuster Children's Publishing Division. Interior illustration from *The Hunter* (2000) by Mary Casanova, illustrated by Ed Young. Illustrations © 2006 Ed Young.

Jess. Illustrations by Robert Papp. (American Girl/Pleasant Company, 2006).

When Jess joins her archeologist parents on a dig in the Central American country of Belize, she makes important discoveries—about the dangers in the jungle and the people who lived there long ago—and about herself.

Cover art for *Jess* (2006) by Mary Casanova. Cover art by Robert Papp. (American Girl/ Pleasant Company). Reprinted with permission.

Interior illustration for *Jess* (2006) by Mary Casanova. Illustration by Robert Papp. (American Girl/Pleasant Company). Reprinted with permission.

Moose Tracks. (Hyperion, 1995).

Seth struggles to save an orphaned moose calf in the northwoods of Minnesota, but finds himself increasingly tangled up with poachers who are threatening not only wildlife, but Seth's family as well. (Fans of Seth and Matt will enjoy reading the sequel, *Wolf Shadows*. My first novel for young readers, this story has been especially popular with reluctant readers and has turned many hard-to-reach boys on to reading.)

Cover art for *Moose Tracks* (1995) by Mary Casanova. Cover art by Kam Mak. (Hyperion). Reprinted with permission.

One-Dog Canoe. Illustrated by Ard Hoyt. (Farrar, Straus and Giroux, 2003).

A girl and her dog set off on a canoe adventure, only to have a beaver, loon, bear, moose, and more ask, "Can I come, too?" When the frog joins the already overloaded canoe, the ride ends in disaster, but the animals work together to help the girl and her dog set off once again.

Jacket design from *One-Dog Canoe* by Mary Casanova, pictures by Ard Hoyt. Text copyright © 2005 by Mary Casanova. Pictures copyright © 2005 by Ard Hoyt. Reprinted by permission of Farrar, Straus and Giroux, LLC.

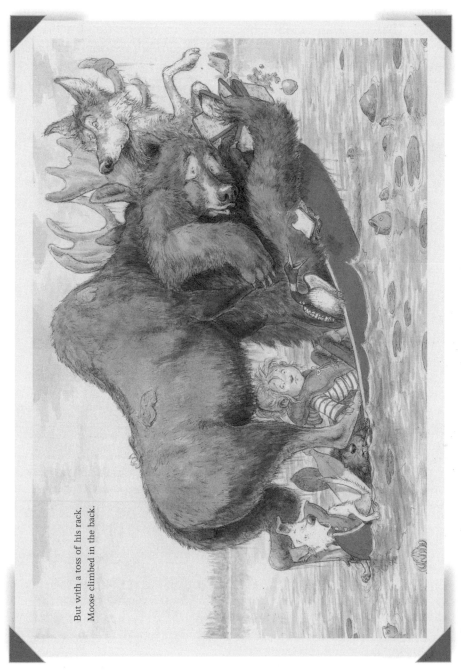

But with a toss of his rack,
Moose climbed in the back.

Interior illustration and text from *One-Dog Canoe* by Mary Casanova, pictures by Ard Hoyt. Text copyright © 2005 by Mary Casanova. Pictures copyright © 2005 by Ard Hoyt. Reprinted by permission of Farrar, Straus and Giroux, LLC.

Riot. (Hyperion, 1996).

Bryan has always looked up to his father, who is also his hockey coach, but when the local strike turns violent and his own dad gets involved, the lines between right and wrong become increasingly blurred. (Based on an actual labor dispute in International Falls, Minnesota, in 1989; while writing *Riot,* I relived difficult emotions related to living through these events.)

Cover art for *Riot* (1996) by Mary Casanova. Cover art by Eric Valesquez. (Hyperion).
Reprinted with permission.

Stealing Thunder. (Hyperion, 1999).

Libby loves riding Thunder at the nearby stable, but when she suspects that Thunder is being mistreated, the only one who seems to hear her concerns is her new friend, Griff—and together they'll risk everything to protect Thunder.

Cover art for *Stealing Thunder* (1999) by Mary Casanova. Cover art by Lisa Desimini. (Hyperion). Reprinted with permission.

When Eagles Fall. (Hyperion, 2002).

Alex has been running from the past ever since she lost her younger brother to cancer. When a storm sweeps Alex and her canoe (and an injured eaglet) off course in the vast wilderness waters of Rainy Lake, she must figure out how to survive, keep Sentry, the eaglet, alive, and in the silence of the wilderness, face her own past.

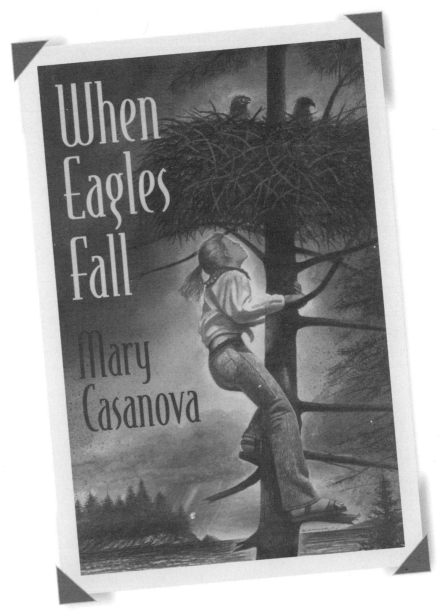

Cover art for *When Eagles Fall* (2002) by Mary Casanova. Cover art by Wendell Minor. (Hyperion). Reprinted with permission.

Wolf Shadows (Hyperion, 1997).

In the frigid northwoods of Minnesota, wolves are on the increase, and Seth is put to the test when wolves come between him and his lifelong friend, Matt.

(A sequel to *Moose Tracks*, but can be read as a separate story as well.)

Cover art for *Wolf Shadows* (1998) by Mary Casanova. Cover art by Dan Brown. (Hyperion). Reprinted with permission.

Frequently Asked Questions: My Answers in Letters

I love trekking to the post office and opening my metal postal box to find fan mail. Granted, e-mail is easier to answer, but postal mail always feels more personal, and when I return home and settle back at my desk, I hope to write equally personal letters in response to readers' questions and comments. Many readers are aspiring writers, and I try to encourage them as other authors have encouraged me.

The following letters are a sampling of the responses I've sent out over the years. Of course, individuals' full names and addresses have been deleted.

A handful of fan letters from the hundreds that arrive yearly via regular mail and e-mail. Credit: From the archives of Mary Casanova. Reprinted with permission.

When a fifth grader wrote me about his interest in writing and asked how to get published, I sent him the following letter...

Dear Jon,

Thanks for sharing your story with me. I like that the story has a problem and a solution, that the character doesn't have to throw a tantrum at the end, and that your story deals with something you know something about—allergic reactions to certain pets.

If you're interested in working in this field, brace yourself for lots of work. Your story is a start, but you will have to learn the craft and really write with polish before you seriously consider publication.

Check out writing organizations or writing groups in your area. Meeting with others who share your dream makes writing less lonely and helps you keep your dream alive as you're learning the craft.

Read everything you can about writing, too. For starters, see if your library has magazines on writing. Two of my favorites are *The Writer* and *Writers' Digest*. I also recommend a book called *WHAT'S YOUR STORY?* by Marion Dane Bauer.

Finally, once you have learned more about the field, buy the latest edition of *The Children's Writers and Illustrators Market* by Writers' Digest Books for a wealth of information about where to send your manuscripts.

All the best, Jon!

Your friend,

Mary Casanova

A fourth-grade girl wrote to me, asking what happens after the ending of *Cécile* and what was the most difficult part of writing that story. Here's how I answered her thoughtful letter...

Dear Taylor,

First, thanks so much for taking the time to write to me!

I'm delighted to know that you enjoyed *Cécile: Gates of Gold*. Like you, I enjoy reading historical fiction, and that's why writing

Cécile's story was such a pleasure. By stepping inside her shoes and imagining life at court, I was almost able to live it (at least in my head). I guess that was my favorite part of the whole process. And since she was a completely fictionalized character, she was the most fun to create. In order to imagine the story, however, I first had to do lots of research; I read many, many books and I spent a week at the palace of Versailles, roaming inside from room to room and outside around the palace grounds. And what a spectacular place it was—and still is!

I'm an animal lover, so it was easier for me to relate to a girl at court who—like me—wouldn't mind taking care of Madame's six dogs. (Oh, Madame really did have all those dogs, too!)

The most difficult scenes to write are the sad scenes. They have to be believable and the reader needs to feel that part of the story. And I agree with you that the saddest scene in the story to me is when young Bretagne passes away. But despite the sad events, I always hope to leave the reader with some hope. That's why, at the story's end, Cécile goes off to St. Cyr. With an education, she has a future—even though as reader you may not know exactly what it will be.

My best writing tip? Keep writing. Keep a journal. And pay attention to the world around you. Oh, and keep reading!

Your friend,

Mary Casanova

Christmas comes early when I receive a packet of letters from a classroom, as was the case with a classroom of third graders who had just finished reading *Stealing Thunder*. I read through each and every illustrated letter and sent one letter in return.

Dear Ms. Conro and students,

Thanks for your letters! To answer some of your questions: Yes, we have animals. We have two dogs (Chester is a beagle and Kito is a chow-mutt cross ... they will be the stars of a book series called *Dog Watch* coming out soon.) I also have a horse—a Morgan mare named Lexi.

On weekends I like to go riding, hiking, and canoeing—anything outside and away from a computer. Though I love to write and to read, I need the outdoors to recharge my soul. We often visit a family cabin outside of Ely near Bearhead Lake State Park, which makes the Ely area one of my favorite places in the whole world.

My husband, Charlie, and I have two college-age kids: Kate and Eric. When they were younger they were my best editors and they gave me feedback on everything I wrote, which was very helpful.

When I was growing up I had an Appaloosa, just like Thunder, but my horse's name was Keema. I loved to go on long rides with him and with a few of my friends who had horses, too. We'd explore fields and forests together. There's nothing better than having a horse as a good friend—except riding together with horse-loving friends!

For *Stealing Thunder*, I was able to draw on all the memories I have of being around horses—especially those involving my five senses. Using the five senses is something that makes anyone's writing stronger and more believable.

Your letters make me think that I should give more thought to writing another horse book—or maybe a sequel to *Stealing Thunder*. Thanks for your enthusiastic words!

Have a great spring and a book-filled summer!

Your friend,

Mary Casanova

A fourth-grade boy wrote and mentioned that he appreciated my use of first-person over third-person point of view (well, not exactly in those words), and here's how I replied ...

Dear Anthony,

Thanks for taking the time to write to me and let me know you enjoyed *Stealing Thunder*. I appreciated hearing that you like when a story is written in third person instead of first person, at least that's what you were referring to when you said, "I don't like how in some books it is in the point of view of the person who is telling it, but in your book you said Libby instead of I." This is one of the points that writers discuss endlessly, and right now I'm changing a whole novel from first person (I) to third person, simply because it suits the story better.

Hockey is a big sport here. You'd fit right in! The only book I've written that includes references to hockey is *Riot*, which you might also enjoy. Though that book isn't about animals, it also has a dog in it named Gretzky. I know you know how I got that name. I'm sure you have your own hockey stories to tell!

Happy Belated Birthday! Happy Reading! It was a great pleasure to hear from you, Anthony!

Your friend,

Mary Casanova

A sixth grader asked how long it takes me to finish a novel and wondered how I got started as a writer. This was my reply...

Dear Tyler,

First, I'm sorry that it has taken me this long to respond to your letter. It first went to my publisher, which is like sending it to a dark hole, and a month or two later it came my way. I'm catching my breath between trips from coast to coast in the past months, so forgive me for not replying sooner!

Thanks for your kind letter. I'm delighted to hear that *Wolf Shadows* is "an awesome book." What a compliment! And that you have a brother by the same name as the main character is fun. By the way, have you read *Moose Tracks*, which comes first? That was my first novel, and it took me four years to write and revise the story before it came out in print. I was learning how to write something of that length. Now most novels take me about a year—sometimes more, sometimes less—and with every book I write many drafts. Revising is hard work, but it makes all the difference. Hearing from readers like you, however, makes the work worthwhile.

I started writing seriously when I was in high school. That's when I fell in love with creating something out of nothing with words. It's an art form that I love, and one that can be learned. For example, one of the things I focus on when it comes to setting is using my five senses and imagining moment by moment what my character might be seeing, hearing, tasting, touching, or smelling. Those are the kind of details that help a setting become real to the reader. (And you can use those same five senses when you write, as well.)

Happy Reading! Happy Writing! It was a great pleasure to hear from you, Tyler. I hope you have a wonderful spring in Michigan! Warmest wishes,

Your friend,

Some fan letters go straight to my heart. When a fifth-grade girl sent a well-written letter complete with illustrations, I cried. She admitted that she had "a hard time making and keeping friends" due to her ADHD, and she said she didn't really expect me to respond since most people ignored her anyway. I saw my earlier self in her words and hoped to encourage her in her talents and in what she was doing right, including maintaining a writers' group of two with a girlfriend who lived several hours away. Here's my rather lengthy reply...

Dear Lauren,

I receive lots of fan letters, but yours is probably one of my favorites. Your letter was honest, straight from the heart, and well written. Plus, I enjoyed your illustrations of a wolf, bunny, flowery vine, heart, unicorns, and young women. You're an artist and a good writer!

Like you, I likely have ADD. Though I've never been diagnosed, my family would nod their heads in agreement. I've learned to focus on the things I do well, like writing, and to keep my life as simple as possible. That means my social life isn't whirling, and my good friends are small in number. I do better if I don't get too spread out. And I'm sharing that in hopes of encouraging you. Focus on your strengths and wonderful abilities and be gracious and forgiving toward yourself when you fall short.

Let me give you an example: Just this morning, I leaned against my 22-year old daughter's painting for the third time. Not just once did I lean against it and rub off the pastels onto the back of my shirt and thereby smudge her large portrait, not just twice, but this was the *third* time in two weeks. Most people wouldn't do that. But it's the kind of thing I do all too frequently. Some things just don't stick in my head. I asked her forgiveness, forgave myself, and moved on. The good lesson in all of this has been that as I learn to be easy and forgiving toward myself, I'm able to be much less judgmental and more forgiving toward others. Everyone, after all, has their own unique challenges.

Thanks for your kind words about my writing. You also mentioned that you have a writing partner. That's wonderful! I'm a strong believer in teaming up with others who share and support your dreams. That's why writers' groups can be so helpful. And a "writers' group" of *two* is exactly how I started. My writing pal lived two hours away from me, so we'd meet halfway once a month to share what we were working on. Without Lois, I'm sure I would have given up and never published my first novel, *Moose Tracks*.

Thanks again for your letter, Lauren! I'll send a copy of this letter to your friend, Angela, since you hoped I would get in touch with her, too. Seems like a good way to do so. (Keep writing, you two!)

May your summer be filled with sweet moments outdoors, with cozy book reading, and with creating. Thanks again for your letter!

Your friend,

Mary Casanova

Some fan letters are short, such as one I received from a second-grade girl who wanted to know what I do for fun. Here's my short letter in return...

Dear Bonnie,

Thanks for your letter! I'm glad to hear you have enjoyed several of my books.

On weekends I like to go riding, hiking, and canoeing—anything outside and away from a computer. Though I love to write and to read, I need the outdoors to recharge my soul.

If you get a chance to read *When Eagles Fall*, please write and let me know what you think of the story. A letter is great, but e-mail is fine, too. You can e-mail me through my Web site at www.marycasanova.com. Thanks for your enthusiastic letter!

Warmest wishes—and Happy Reading!

Your friend,

Mary Casanova

When letters come scrawled in big letters, I try to reply with a style appropriate to the age of my reader. A first grader wanted to know who ate the sandwich in *One-Dog Canoe*, and here was my answer. . . .

Dear Justin,

I'm so pleased to hear from you and to know that you loved *One-Dog Canoe*. To answer your question, I'm not sure exactly who ate the sandwich in the story. Some things are left to the imagination of the reader!

The illustrator added an extra touch to the story. On the back flap copy, look who is in the picnic basket. Maybe the frog snuck along by hopping into the basket when everyone was saying good-bye. It adds a little more fun to the story and makes me wonder, too, if the girl and her dog have a stowaway in the basket as they set off again!

Happy Reading!

Your friend,

Mary Casanova

Some teachers use my books every year in literature circles or as class read-alouds. A dedicated teacher in Michigan shares *Riot* with her sixth graders every March, and every April or May I reply to several of her students' letters that come my way. Here's how I replied one year. . .

Dear Terra, Ellie, Samantha, and Adam,

Thanks so much for your letters about *Riot*. Since you've sent them, I've been on the road to Missouri, Montana, and Nevada— even so, I apologize for not responding more quickly.

You seemed to all like the ending even though it is a bit ambiguous. Some readers want the ending tied up with a big red bow, but this didn't seem like the kind of story that could be so easily summed up. Ellie wrote: "I realized what it was really about— keeping a family together when the times were tough. You learn about trust and how to handle those bad situations." Similarly, Samantha shared: "Nobody's perfect, not even parents . . . families need to stick together." As to the ending, she added, "there is more to tell ... when Bryan's dad gets out of jail, he and Bryan will become closer." That is my hope, too. A hopeful ending, something learned along the way, and work to be done ahead toward the family's and community's healing.

Another book of mine that you might want to read that parallels *Riot* in some ways is *Curse of a Winter Moon*, set in the mid-1500s in France. Different issues, yet a character who struggles with some of the mob mentality of his community and has to sort through it for himself.

Adam, I hope I can return to Houghton again before long, too! As to a sequel, Terra, I once thought I might return to this story, but I'm feeling finished with it now, even though the ending opens up into sequel possibilities. More books on the way, however, without a doubt!

Over the summer, pick up *When Eagles Fall* if you want to read a contemporary survival story set where I live on Rainy Lake. You'll have a better idea of what I call my "backyard" and my favorite island on the whole lake.

Thank you for your letters!

Your fan,

Mary Casanova

And here's how I replied another year regarding the same book. The book might stay the same, but the questions and comments are always different.

Dear Rachel, Nikka, and Emily,

Thanks you for fan your letters about *Riot*. Because some of your questions are similar, I'm going to write you all one letter. I hope you don't mind.

I love my work as a writer: I love creating, I love editing, and I love hearing from readers such as you all. That said, writing is also hard, hard work. After I write a story and revise it over and over and over again, I send it off into the world and move on to the next book. I never go back and read one of my books cover to cover.

The day the riot took place, I knew I would eventually write about the events that happened. I wasn't ready to tackle the story, however, until five years later. That's when I interviewed locals, including the sheriff (who let me watch spliced videotape footage from the event), and reviewed newspaper coverage. If you go to my Web site you'll be able to hear some footage from locals looking back on that day via Minnesota Public Radio. Though I had threats that something would happen to my husband's business if I wrote the story, I went ahead and wrote *Riot* and tried to tell the story as fairly as I could. The book went on to win several awards. No negative repercussions followed—thank God.

Yes, I have written other books, which you can check out at my Web site: www.marycasanova.com. I have seven novels published and many more books coming.

You might try *Curse of a Winter Moon* as a book that's similar in *Riot* in that it looks at mob behavior, but it also delves into superstitions about werewolves back in the mid-1500s in France.

Thank you for your letters! Keep thinking. Keep reading!

Warmest wishes,

Mary Casanova

One fifth-grade boy wrote to ask where I get my story ideas and the endings for my stories. Here's how I responded:

August 10, 2005

Dear Clint,

I just received your March letter from my publisher and I apologize that you've waited so long for a reply. Thanks for sending your school photo, too, as it helps me see you more clearly in my mind.

I'm so glad that you and your dad enjoyed reading *Wolf Shadows* together! That's great that you can share a love of books and the outdoors. Have you read books by Gary Paulsen? His book *Hatchet* inspired me to write my first novel for young readers, *Moose Tracks*, which you said you enjoyed reading in class.

As to your question—how do I think of my ideas or think of endings? I often start with a question in the back of my mind, such as what do I think about taking an animal's life? And maybe I start asking more questions, such as what's the difference between poaching and responsible hunting? I start paying attention to ideas around me. When I was writing *Moose Tracks* and volunteering on a reservation in northern Minnesota, I started to appreciate that the Ojibwe hunters traditionally thank an animal for giving its life—seeing all life as a gift. Certainly, that helped shape the ending of *Moose Tracks*, where Seth regrets wastefully killing the rabbit in the opening of the story and returns to that spot in the woods at the end of the book to thank the rabbit for giving its life. I grew up with a family of deer hunters, but I do not hunt. By writing *Moose Tracks*, I discovered that what matters to me is a spirit of humility, not arrogance, when we walk through the woods—and through life.

That's a much longer answer than you probably were looking for! But writing stories is a complicated process and everything we think about, everything we experience, flows into the stories we write. Even the stories you write, Clint.

Hope you've had a great summer! Happy Reading—and writing!

Your friend,

P.S. I will be visiting some schools in Rochester this school year. If I come to your school, please introduce yourself.

I replied to a letter from my "# 1 Fan" with some words of encouragement about her own writing abilities:

August 11, 2005

Dear Shava,

I loved visiting your school and the whole Kalispell area in Montana. You live in one of the most beautiful places in the world with Flathead Lake, Whitefish Lake, and the surrounding mountains. Lucky, lucky you!

We certainly share a lot in common: we both grew up in big families, we both love the outdoors (and horses), and we both love to write. You said that you're not good with ideas and word choice, but I disagree. You wrote "It must be fun lying out on the dock with your laptop and dipping your feet in the water." I loved reading this. I could feel the water on my toes and the warm dock. You were able to imagine a setting and put yourself inside a character and hint at the five senses. I say, keep writing, Shava.

Thanks for telling me that all of my books are "filled with con-flict and suspense" and that when you finished reading my books you "wanted them to go on and on." I take that as a compliment. My hope as a writer is that the reader will care enough about the main character to keep turning the pages, and if that's the case, then (as with any really good book) the reader is reluctant to get to the last page.

Keep reading, keep writing, and keep dreaming!

Your friend,

Mary Casanova

PART TWO

The Stories Behind the Stories

Adventure Novels

MOOSE TRACKS

Moose Tracks, in short, is about twelve-year-old Seth Jacobsen's struggle to save an orphaned moose calf from poachers. I'm often asked, "Where did the inspiration come from for your first novel?" Looking back over a decade, I realize it sprang from a number of sources. The first was an image.

Though I've seen moose in the wild, I had never been close to a six-month-old moose calf. Part of my research for *Moose Tracks* included a special visit to see one of the orphaned moose calves at the Minnesota Zoo. The zookeeper allowed me to get "up close" and to observe the calf's fur, build, and behavior. Credit: From the archives of Mary Casanova. Reprinted with permission.

One early fall, a blizzard hit unexpectedly. From the warmth of my house, I looked out my backyard window. Wind whipped treetops and pelted my house and backyard with snow. Swallows flitted frantically, struggling to find shelter, their coattail feathers askew in the gale force. Desperate, the swallows clustered at the birdhouse, but the shelter was already full. Not a single additional bird could squeeze in. Still, swallows kept flying to the birdhouse, only to be turned away. I felt helpless, wishing I could do something to save the swallows.

That initial image of swallows caught in a blizzard without shelter moved me and led me to ponder possibilities for a novel. In Chapter Two, Seth scans his backyard during an early fall storm where swallows are taking shelter in a birdhouse. In my original draft I devoted a couple of paragraphs to the swallows, but in countless later drafts, that initial compelling image was reduced to one or two sentences of description, woven in with the rest of the setting. So what was it in that initial moment looking out my own window at swallows trying to take shelter that led to writing a novel about poaching and moose? Is it possible that whole novels spring from such moments when we focus and time stands still? When we want to help, but can't? When we struggle with our own moral dilemma? After all, I was cozy and warm, completely secure in the storm. But outside, those swallows struggled for their lives, vulnerable to the elements.

I started to brainstorm for parallel story lines. What if a child needed shelter from a storm? What if a Native American girl needed to come in out of the cold? I pondered what the family might be like who would take in such a girl. Perhaps the father is a game warden, the mother a social worker, the son... In the early drafts of the story, I did include such a girl in the story, but when my editor asked for the first rewrite, she said that I had so much going on that I could do a separate novel someday about the Native American girl, which I have since decided not to write after volunteering at the Bois Fort Reservation school to teach writing. I realized that a whole lifetime would not be enough for me to truly step inside the Ojibwe culture and write authentically from that viewpoint. I took my editor's advice, cut the Native American girl from the story, and focused on my main character, Seth.

Seth, like one of my nephews when I was writing this book, struggles to find his place in his changing family. His stepfather has always treated him like his own son, but with a new baby on the way—a biological child to both of his parents—Seth begins to doubt his worth. His outer struggle of saving a moose calf from poachers and proving his self-worth comes out of his need to prove himself to his stepfather and to gain a greater sense of acceptance and a place in his family.

When I was starting out, I met published authors who critiqued my work and gave me suggestions. At the first SCBWI conference that I attended, I was fortunate to have a Newbery author, Avi, critique my early draft of *Moose Tracks*. I also met fellow writer Jane Kurtz there. We have been writing friends ever since. Recently when I was signing at an ALA conference, Avi joked with me, "Friends don't let friends write."

At the time my first draft of *Moose Tracks* was critiqued at the SCBWI conference, I had Seth going into the woods, finding moose tracks, and running into poachers. It was Avi who asked, "Is it always black and white in the real world?" Or at least that's what I remember him asking. He encouraged me to think about the gray areas, the areas in life where we struggle. And right away I knew that he was right. My own brothers could do things to frogs, like blow them out of the handlebars of a bike with a firecracker. And I loved my brothers and knew they had redeeming qualities as well.

I went back home and rewrote the story again, this time starting the story differently. To prove himself, Seth goes into the woods with his friend, Matt, to shoot a rabbit for its rabbit's foot. When he later encounters poachers in the story, Seth must weigh his own actions against those of the poachers. The story has a plot and a subplot, an outer struggle and an inner struggle.

When I speak, I often demonstrate with my arms the large, heavy box that holds all of the drafts for *Moose Tracks*. It was the first story that I'd ever written of that length (over one hundred pages, which at the time was daunting!). I struggled with the plot and with the basics of writing. The things that I understand more organically now, I barely understood then, from point of view, to escalating conflict, to using sensory and specific details. But I was passionate about learning, and I believed in my bones that I had a story to share. I kept revising.

Readers over the years have shared heartwarming e-mails and letters with me about this first book. A librarian in Maine told me that "It's being passed around from hockey mom to hockey mom because their sons (hockey players) are reading it!" Teachers who work with struggling readers tell me often that *Moose Tracks* is the book that will hook and hold a hard-to-reach reader, usually a boy, but once he's finished the book he's ready to read. Parents tell me that their third, fourth, fifth, sixth, seventh, or eighth grader will read *Moose Tracks* and that it's the first book they've enjoyed reading cover to cover.

Hearing such feedback is hugely satisfying for me, especially since I began with two goals: to write a story that mattered and to write a story that kids couldn't put down. I knew intuitively that if I could hook boys as readers, I would find plenty of girls as readers as well. I identified with the restless reader, the one who would rather be outside being active, and so I tried to write the kind of story that would have held my attention, page by page, right to the very end. I worked on making the opening page intriguing, and I ended each chapter on a high note of tension.

Recently, a bookstore owner e-mailed me to tell me that there was a 12-year-old boy who had a brain tumor and was in the hospital. She said the boy's teacher had come into the bookstore to find the boy's "favorite book they'd read in class." It was *Moose Tracks*, and the boy had requested the book so his father could read it to him at his bedside. I was humbled, and grateful for the opportunity to send the boy and his family a letter of sympathy and also the book's sequel, *Wolf Shadows*, on audiotape.

Still, why write about a boy struggling to save a moose calf? The easiest answer, the one I often talk about, is that I was writing about something I loved and something that troubled me. I have always loved wildlife, and seeing a moose in the wild is always exciting. They're huge, almost prehistoric looking. My grandfather used to tell a story about how once when he was out deer hunting, a bull moose charged him and he was forced to climb up the nearest tree for safety (a scene quite similar to the scene depicted on the cover of my book). I was also writing something that troubled me—namely, poaching.

Our local newspaper reported poachers arrested with the gall bladders of black bears, an alleged aphrodisiac in high demand in Asia (where the bear population has been hit hard). Laws are made to protect basic wildlife populations so that these natural resources will be around for generations to come. I was upset about the reported incidents of local poaching and thought there might be a story worth exploring.

Beneath the issue of poaching is another image—and question—from my childhood. During hunting season, deer carcasses hung from the rafters of the garage. I grew up with avid deer hunters—my grandfathers and my father were hunters—and my husband and son hunt on occasion as well. *Moose Tracks* was my way of exploring the difference between responsible hunting and poaching.

I love watching deer nibble on a field of grass and leap gracefully away when they sense an intruder. Yet how can I be against deer hunting when I eat venison—and still do? If I were a vegetarian, then I might have written something like *Bambi*, instead of *Moose Tracks*. It wasn't that I was against hunting. It was something else. I thought about the bravado when my father and brothers returned from deer hunting, and their back-slapping and high-fiving. It seemed all about the hunter, while the animal whose tongue hung coldly out of its mouth was just a thing. A trophy.

By writing *Moose Tracks*, I began exploring my own feelings about hunting, poaching, and taking an animal's life. An Ojibwe hunter offers thanks to the animal for giving its life—offers thanks to the Great Spirit. Every life is a gift. This was the attitude I was missing when I witnessed the aftermath of my father's and brothers' hunts. To my dad's credit, he always preached to never waste an animal's life. "Only shoot what you plan to eat," he'd said. For me, it's not that taking an animal's life is wrong, especially if the hunter is abiding by the law and not being wasteful. It's the hunter's attitude toward life that matters, a sense of reverence and belonging, rather than dominating just to prove one's own worth. Real power lies in humility, Seth finally discovers, not in an outward show of strength.

Every story starts from a different place and leads me up mountains and through valleys. Like the swallows that tugged at my compassion and offered an image for *Moose Tracks*, I am moved to write about what I love and especially about what troubles or *haunts* me.

WOLF SHADOWS

When I finished *Moose Tracks*, I thought I was done writing about Seth Jacobsen and his best friend, Matt. On the completion of my second novel, however, I took greater interest in the issue of a growing wolf population and the resulting conflicts with people. And where else could I better play out differing attitudes about wolves than with Seth and Matt?

Again, what I love became my inspiration—this time, wolves. Just last week, my husband and I were driving down a remote logging trail and a lanky year-old wolf gazed at us from the middle of the grassy road, then, after several seconds, fled away into the shadowy forest. From remote stretches of highway, we often spot lone wolves and once, a wolf pack pulling at a freshly hit deer. From ice roads on Rainy Lake (the lake truly freezes with a foot of ice that trucks drive across in winter), we've witnessed wolves crossing from island to island. When we're out skiing, we often come across wolf tracks and wolf scat—evidence that wolves are nearby—and enjoy knowing that wolves are sharing the forest with us.

One February day, I found an image that led me to write *Wolf Shadows.* I was cross-country skiing with my family on the Black Bay trails in Voyageur's National Park. The sun beamed from a true blue sky, chickadees flitted between pine boughs, wolf tracks dotted a beaver's lodge blanketed with fresh snow, and ravens were courting, calling back and forth in gravelly voices, sounding like aging country-western singers. Our skis glided through the powdery snow, following ski ruts through the woods. We came around a bend and stopped abruptly. There in front of us was a wide swath of blood in the snow. Wolf tracks and deer tracks, along with tawny deer fur, were scattered everywhere. Only a deer hoof and a deer leg bone remained.

Winters might be cold in International Falls, but that's no reason to stay inside. Here, daughter Kate (at thirteen) gets ready for a cross-country ski competition. Credit: From the archives of Mary Casanova. Reprinted with permission.

This was the first—and only time—that I have come across a fresh wolf kill. It shocked me out of my romantic moment of skiing through the woods that day. The wolves had attacked, killed for food, and left nothing behind. I was pulled from my modern view of wilderness as a recreation area to the larger reality: life is a cycle of beginnings and ends. The wolf played its part as predator, keeping the deer herd culled by preying most often on the sick and injured, leaving the stronger breeding stock to survive. Though my stomach lurched at the wolf kill, I skied on, humbled by reality, by the image, and left to ponder.

Wolves and humans in close proximity create conflict. Before wolves were protected through the Endangered Species Act, they had been shot, trapped, and poisoned until their numbers were greatly threatened. After nearly a quarter of a decade of federal protection, the wolf population in Minnesota has made a tremendous rebound with numbers estimated at somewhere between two thousand and three thousand. Most of those wolves live in the northern regions, the less populated regions, of the state.

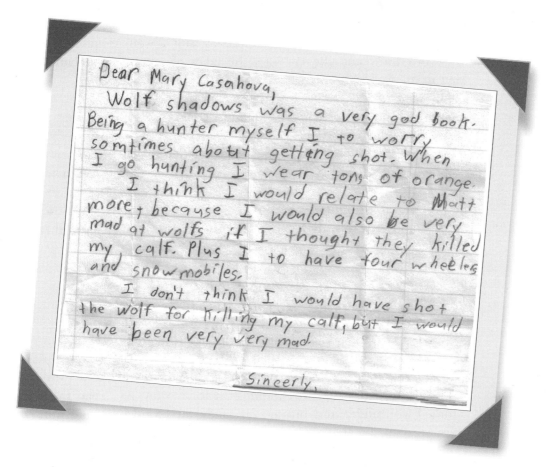

Dear Mary Casanova,
Wolf shadows was a very god book.
Being a hunter myself I to worry
somtimes about getting shot. When
I go hunting I wear tons of orange.
   I think I would relate to Matt
more, because I would also be very
mad at wolfs if I thought they killed
my calf. Plus I to have four wheeles
and snowmobiles.
   I don't think I would have shot
the wolf for killing my calf, but I would
have been very very mad.

                    Sincerly,

The topic of hunting in *Moose Tracks* and *Wolf Shadows* resonates with many readers, especially boys. Credit: From the archives of Mary Casanova. Reprinted with permission.

Living on the northern border, I have a sense of the conflicts that erupt over wolves. There are people who love wolves and fully support their protection and our nearby national park. Others, often descendants of families who have had roots in the north for generations, feel that the land is "theirs" and that wolves threaten the deer population that they value hunting. Farmers who lose livestock do not appreciate wolves attacking their animals. The stable owner where I board my horse witnessed two wolves in the pasture approaching the horses and shouted at them to leave, which they did.

What if, I began wondering, Matt's family viewed wolves as a threat to their livestock and to "their deer." What if Seth, who has learned a little humility and respect for wildlife after his encounter with poachers, takes a broader view of wolves? What if these two lifelong friends have a conflict over wolves that leads to a life-threatening situation? And indeed, the circumstances do turn deadly. Matt believes he's lost a bottle-fed prize calf to wolf predation and on the first day of deer hunting takes revenge on a wolf. Seth is outraged that his friend has shot a wolf, violating his own sense of ethics—and the law—and he takes off, unwittingly abandoning Matt in the woods, unaware that a blizzard is brewing.

By writing *Wolf Shadows*, I stepped into opposing viewpoints to better understand a thorny environmental issue. I still believe that wolves have their valued place in wilderness, yet I have more compassion for those who lose livestock—or pets—to their carnivorous and territorial neighbor, *Canus lupus*. If my compassion can stretch through writing such a story, then I hope that readers, too, will be taken on a journey beyond initial assumptions to a more in-depth probing of an issue. And above all, I hope that they experience a taste of the wilderness through an engaging adventure story.

STEALING THUNDER

One day, a newspaper article jumped out at me. Several men had been arrested for maiming or killing horses in an insurance scam. These individuals had worked around expensive horses and were willing, out of greed, to destroy them—just for money. As I read the story, I fumed with anger and outrage. It made my blood boil, and immediately, recognizing that strong emotion about a topic often fuels me to explore something further in fiction, I cut out the article and put it in a file I keep called "Story Ideas." A few years later, that article started to morph into a plot for *Stealing Thunder*.

Thunderbird, "Thunder" for short, is an Appaloosa, fashioned after the horse I had when I was growing up, named Keema. And though my Appaloosa had never been abused, I feel compassion for horses that suffered mistreatment. Writers are often told, "Write what you know." With my love of horses and having had horses when I was younger, it was natural that I would want to write a horse story. When I announced my newest project to my daughter (Kate was about eleven at the time and not much interested in horses), she said, "Mom, I'm not going to read this manuscript. Horse stories are *so* boring!"

"Well, then my challenge," I replied, "is to write a good story that happens to have horses in it. I'll try to write a book that even nonhorse lovers might enjoy."

Stealing Thunder has been nominated by kids in several states as a favorite book for state book award master lists. Scholastic featured it in their book clubs and book fairs. And though the book came out several years ago, I continue to get fan mail from enthusiastic readers.

Granted, many of the readers are fans of horses—and that's fine with me—and many are readers are just enjoying an adventure story.

I'd written three novels up until that point, and *Moose Tracks*, *Riot*, and *Wolf Shadows* all featured boys as main characters. I thought it would be relatively easy, therefore, to finally slip into the shoes of a female protagonist for a change. What I found halfway through the first draft, however, was that I was completely stuck. Karen Severson, one of my local writers' group members and a therapist by training, listened to me as I reached the end of what I had hoped would be a dramatic, effective chapter.

"Mary," she asked gently. "Why won't you let this character have a voice?"

I was dumbstruck by the surgical exactness of her question. Indeed, when I thought my character would stand up for herself, she disappeared into a corner and had become voiceless. Cowardly. Yet I hadn't realized it until I'd read from my manuscript. Karen was right. Why couldn't I let my character have a voice?

"Um, I don't really know," I finally answered. "But I'd better figure it out."

For the next week or two, I journaled intensively. Though I felt I was at the time, in Maslow's definition of a well-adjusted adult, "fully actualized," I had to figure out what in my upbringing and childhood was keeping me stuck in my novel. I had to look at my training to be "nice," to be "good hearted," and to be a "Christian" at all times. As an adult, I had learned to speak up and to speak out, to have a voice. But writing through the eyes of a twelve-year-old girl, I had unwittingly slipped back into more of who I was at that age. I had hated conflict. The louder someone got, like my father in one of his wrathful storms, the quieter I became. The more conflict escalated in my family, the more I retreated. No wonder, then, that as I was writing dramatic scenes in *Stealing Thunder*, I found Libby, my main character, retreating.

In my original family, my brothers went on goose- and deer-hunting expeditions and fishing trips to Canada. As a girl, however, I was not included on these all-male adventures. My sisters and I always stayed home to help Mom, who certainly always needed help with toddlers and babies in bassinets. I wanted to be helpful, but I also longed for the outdoor experiences my brothers had. In my first three novels, then, I had been able to allow my male characters to be assertive. I had been able to vicariously speak up through them, to take risks and stand up to conflict. What a surprise that in my early drafts about Libby, my main character, all that courage had dwindled away! In my journals I expressed my frustration and anger at the voicelessness I'd felt growing up, my timidity in the face of confrontation. Finally, I returned to my novel and released my character from her author-imposed chains.

After reading the next draft of *Stealing Thunder*, my editor, Julia Richardson, then at Hyperion, said something like, "It's great that your character is now more assertive. But she needs to grow from the beginning to the end. Right now she starts out with all the answers. There needs to be an arc in her growth and self-awareness."

So I returned again to the novel, this time realizing that it was fine if my character started out more like the twelve-year old I had been who struggled to find her voice and to speak out. But in this draft, Libby must grow. Despite her hesitation to confront the abusive owner of her favorite horse, Thunderbird, Libby takes small and important steps toward self-growth and action. By story's end, Libby learns to use her voice. And I learned something new about myself the writing process.

In writing *Stealing Thunder*, I loved remembering the sensory details associated with stepping into the barn, feeding a horse grain and hay, saddling up, and heading out on a trail ride. Those details came easily to me.

I had not expected a character to step out of nowhere into *Stealing Thunder*. Griff makes his debut in Chapter Four at the pond. He hadn't been in my original plans. I was writing an early draft with Libby keeping watch in a tree, when suddenly, a boy her age steps into the picture. In those writing moments when something unexpected presents, I have a choice: stay with my original ideas, or let the scene roll, much like a movie camera, and see what happens. Had I needed to maintain absolute control over my plot, I would never have gotten to know Griff, who comes from a troubled background and has gotten in a fair share of trouble himself, but at heart he's a good kid. And, importantly for Libby, he's the only one who seems to hear her concerns about the welfare of the neighbor's horse, Thunderbird. The adults don't seem to hear her, but Griff does. In him, she finds a friend and an ally, and together they go to whatever lengths they must to save Thunder from mistreatment, including stealing the horse away to safety.

WHEN EAGLES FALL

For two days on Rainy Lake, I was part of a research team, squatting on the ground and holding the legs of six-week-old, nearly adult-size eaglets. While biologists took measurements, blood samples, and such, I gripped the eaglet's legs: waxy, yellow, and warm as its heartbeat pulsed through my hands. I could never have dreamed that such incredible opportunities could be part of my research; and I needed to know everything I could about eagles and the work of eagle researchers. The biologists banded eaglets at over a dozen different nests, and I absorbed every moment.

Three main threads form the plot for *When Eagles Fall*: eagles, cancer, and kids in trouble. When Alex loses her younger brother to cancer, her family falls apart, too, and Alex starts running around with the wrong crowd. Because Alex gets in trouble, she's sent to spend time with her father, an eagle researcher in northern Minnesota, and suddenly finds herself lost with an injured eaglet on the vast waters of Rainy Lake. Not only must she survive and try to keep the eaglet alive, but in the silence of the wilderness, she's forced to finally confront the pain surrounding the loss of her brother.

My love for eagles comes easily. When I sip my morning coffee, I often watch them soar past my house and across the bay, much to the chagrin of the seagull population, who send sentries out to harass the mighty eagles. From our houseboat, we watched a seagull swoop in front of us, grab a fish in its talons, and fly off to the nearest perch. One frigid February day, I watched two eagles tumble together from the sky and fall to the shelf of ice below, their talons entwined. They released their talons from their freefall tumble, disentangled from each other, and landed safely on the ice, only to rise again to the sky and start the process all over.

When I mentioned this sky-tumbling behavior to one of the biologists, he said, "You saw that?! In all my years of working with eagles, I've never witnessed that behavior. That's their courtship dance."

I felt just a bit smug.

For two days, we went by boat to twelve nests. At each site, whether on an island or deep inland, Dr. Bill Bowerman climbed to an eagle's nest at the top of a large pine. He used climbing ropes and spiked boots, and the process left him sweaty and covered with debris from nest matter and tree sap. Once he was at the nest, he used a cane-like device to hook an eaglet by its leg, bagged it in an orange nylon bag, and sent the bird carefully by rope to the team that waited below. Then, within the scope of an hour,

Dr. Bill Bowerman, a leading eagle researcher, scaled towering pines with climbing equipment to reach the nests. Credit: From the archives of Mary Casanova. Reprinted with permission.

the eaglet was returned to its nest and off we went again, leaving the circling adults to return to their important job of feeding and protecting their young.

I situated part of the novel at my favorite nesting island: Skipper Rock Island. As a family we've stayed there overnight many times with our houseboat, tucking into the shelter of the island's horseshoe-shaped bay. We wait until late summer to visit, however, after the eaglets fledge, and the park service announces in mid-August that the island can be visited without disturbing the nesting pair of eagles. The rocks along the shores of that island are flat and round—perfect skipping stones to toss across the water. If readers want to see the island where Alex climbs a skinny tree to the nest, it's out there, just to the east of Dryweed Island, and undoubtedly inhabited by eagles.

I couldn't have written *When Eagles Fall* without doing hands-on research. If Alex's father was going to be an eagle researcher, I needed to see what they do. I needed to know the size, the eye color, the behavior of the eaglets. It was on the last nest of the last day that my plot began to grow. Dr. Bowerman had sent down one eaglet to the team, and he planned to band the remaining eaglet in the nest. When he used the metal cane-like device to pull the eaglet to him, however, something went wrong. The eaglet twisted and Bill heard a "snap."

"Oh, no," he called down. "Send up another bag."

Top: Though I thought I would simply be taking notes and photographs for my research, I was given the task of holding the legs of nearly adult-size eaglets. Bottom: The biologists put baseball caps on the eaglets' heads to quiet them down while they took blood samples and measurements, and put metal identification bands around their ankles before returning them to their nests. Credit: From the archives of Mary Casanova. Reprinted with permission.

He lowered the eaglet to the ground, quickly descended from the tree, and, with tears in his eyes, explained that the eaglet's leg was broken. Dr. Bowerman is a highly skilled and experienced researcher, with over twenty years of experience, and he was devastated. He temporarily bandaged the eaglet's leg, we all boated back to the mainland, and I emptied one of my manuscript boxes of its contents. I lined the box with a towel, added air holes, and then we shipped the box off to the Raptor Center in St. Paul, Minnesota. With that incident, I was reminded how the best intentions can go wrong. Even when we think we're doing something helpful, things can backfire. In *When Eagles Fall*, therefore, Alex also is trying to do something helpful. She climbs a tree to remove a dangerous fishing lure from a nest, but one of the eaglets backs up and falls, injuring its wing. I drew on all of my research, and especially on the emotions of what had happened on our last day of banding eaglets.

The other strand in this novel is cancer. I lost my mother-in-law, Rita Casanova, to breast cancer when she was forty-seven years old. I lost my mentor and friend, Pam Conrad, at about the same age to breast cancer as well. Though I didn't write about the loss of these important women in my life, I chose instead to write about the loss of a younger brother to cancer. The circumstances from real life and my story are different, but the emotions are similar: loss, grief, guilt, acceptance. . .

The final source of inspiration, besides eagles and cancer, was my desire to explore why kids and teens (and even adults) get in trouble. When kids or teens act out, as Alex does when she experiments with drinking and finds herself in the hospital, I believe that their behavior is a way of dealing with the pain in their lives. When seemingly good kids suddenly take a sharp left or right turn in sixth, seventh, or eighth grade, I always wonder what pain or hurt are they avoiding? By exploring Alex's journey in *When Eagles Fall*, I was better able to untangle her behavior from her feelings and set her on a path to inner healing. Alex finds herself lost, struggling to survive, and finally, away from her buzzing and active life in San Jose, California, she's forced to face the painful loss of her brother.

Sometimes life, like a satisfying novel, offers a happy ending. After the injured eaglet was shipped to the Raptor Center, the bird made a speedy recovery. Exactly one month later, I went to the International Falls Airport to meet up with a Raptor Center biologist, the crated eaglet, Dr. Bill Bowerman (who flew back to Minnesota from North Carolina), and Lee Grim, local naturalist and park service biologist. The wooden crate was labeled in large letters: EAGLE. We boated back to the island of the eaglet's birth, where its parents circled overhead and its sibling was resting on a tree stump.

"Good," Bill said. "This means they're still feeding their young."

He climbed to the treetop with the orange nylon bag, slipped the bag from around the eaglet's head, and let the eaglet peer out at the world again from its treetop nest. "I've never seen an eaglet look so surprised," Bill said later. "It's as if he was thinking, 'Hey! How'd I get back home?'"

I loved being part of that eaglet's homecoming. I trust it has grown to adulthood and is out there now, soaring above the endless islands and inlets of Rainy Lake.

MORE ADVENTURE NOVELS

The Pelican Games

After nearly a century, pelicans are returning and making a comeback to Rainy Lake, here on the Minnesota-Canadian border. With a wingspan of nine feet, they circle slowly overhead, then descend and land gracefully on our bay. At first we were lucky to see two or three of these mighty birds; this year I counted a flock of forty-two, fishing in formation.

One day as I observed two dozen pelicans floating along, heads tilted, my elderly neighbor started up his fishing boat and headed out into the flock. He ran down the birds until each and every pelican was forced to take flight. Once he'd cleared the bay, he returned to the dock, smug as a little boy.

I was fuming. I marched over, hands on my hips.

The moment he turned off his motor, I said, "I am *not* okay with that."

"I know you're not," he said, "but I don't care."

"I know you don't care, but the bay does not belong to you." I explained how I loved seeing the birds and said that he didn't have a right to run them down. Not to mention the questionable legality of his actions.

We went back and forth about the pelicans. He felt they were only going to grow in number until they ate all the fish in the lake. I believed that the pelicans had a place in the ecosystem and that they had once been part of this eighty-mile lake before commercial fishermen took matters into their own hands and eliminated the pelicans at the turn of the twentieth century.

"I won't do it again," he finally said. "But they just make me so mad!"

As a writer, everything becomes story material. I marched home, explained to Charlie and Kate about my little confrontation.

"I'm proud of you, Mom," Kate said. She knows that I'm slow to anger and that it takes quite a lot of courage for me to speak out.

"I think I'll write a story," I said, "called The Pelican Wars."

The novel I'm writing now is about an eleven-year-old boy and his opinionated grandfather. In the opening chapter, Grandpa Harry sends pelicans flying from Reel 'Em In Bay. As the story progresses and other characters step onto the stage, I'm retitling it to *THE PELICAN GAMES*. My real-life encounter with my neighbor was an emotional springboard into a story. But once started, each story takes on a life of its own.

Besides, I can't use only that afternoon encounter to keep me fueled through a whole novel, especially when the day after our show down over pelicans my neighbor heard my lawnmower hit something hard—crack!—and stop running. He was quick to come over, diagnose that I'd killed my mower, and help me figure out what size mower blade I needed to order.

Like life, novels are *not* black and white. At their best, they mirror the complex hues of real life—of what it means to be human. I may start a novel in the heat of strong emotion or opinion, yet it's through the writing that I stretch my own limited thinking and awareness. It's through the writing that I try on the shoes of another character and his or her viewpoint. If the story is true enough, honest enough, then this grappling with different characters and conflict leads to the main character's eventual growth, understanding, and empathy.

Songwriter Chris Koza wrote in one of his songs, "Empathy doesn't occur in a vacuum ..." Neither can characters grow and change without conflict. It's an essential ingredient of story. But taking conflict and using it toward a higher purpose—that's magic.

Going Downhill Fast

As with most families I know, mental illness has cropped up in my family. I never gave this issue much thought until bipolar disease arose in some of my extended family members in their adult years.

Good people get sick, and good people get mentally ill, too. Mental illness can be devastating to families and—if not treated—dangerous. It's one thing as an adult to confront mental illness in other adults. But what happens, I've often wondered, if the adult who shepherds a child is mentally ill ... or getting ill? I know I will write a novel that deals with this question, and so far, the one that seems to be on the back burner is a novel set in Montana, in a setting that I love—the Rocky

Mountains, with downhill skiing/snowboarding. And I'll likely combine this love with something that troubles me, sometimes scares me to my core. Mental illness.

What if a twelve-year-old finds himself faced with a parent getting mentally ill? It's the parent he has learned to trust from a young age, but suddenly he's being uprooted and moved across the country to Montana. How might the story unfold? What challenges would this character face? And, most difficult of all, what can a twelve-year-old really do in the face of mental illness? I'm interested in what happens when the roles of parent and child are suddenly reversed.

Stories more often seem to find me than that I actively go seeking them. This issue is one that nags at me, prods my subconscious, and won't quite let go. For that reason, I know that eventually, I'll have to simply write the story that "wants to be written." And that makes the whole process rather amazing to me. I'm in control as a writer, but I'm not in control. My prayer is usually "Lord, help! I can't write this on my own!" To my amazement, time and again, my simple prayers are answered. I get what I need when I'm doing research; I get encouragement for an idea just when I need it; and the right fact or thread presents itself just when I think I teeter on the edge of getting stuck. For answered prayers, and for the mysterious Divine in my life—for overall mental health—I say, "Thank you, thank you, thank you."

Historical Novels

RIOT

Writing my second novel, *Riot*, took courage. Not only was I writing about events that took place in International Falls, Minnesota, but while writing the story, I encountered verbal threats. I heard things through the grapevine, such as "If she's going to write that book, then we're not going to her husband's business," and "If she writes about what happened, we're going to vote with our wallets." In other words, if I wrote *Riot*, my husband's local insurance agency could be targeted. At that time in my writing career, his income provided food, shelter, and housing for our family. I didn't take the threats lightly.

What kind of event could lead to such threats? A heated labor dispute. In 1989 International Falls made the local and national news when a wildcat strike and riot erupted. The local paper mill had decided to expand, and for two years they employed primarily nonunion workers to build a huge addition to their plant. International Falls is a strong union town, and this corporate decision to hire largely out-of-state workers who weren't card-carrying union members infuriated the rank and file. Inflamed editorials filled the newspaper. Merchants who sold items to nonunion workers were boycotted. Car tires were slashed. Windshields were bashed in. This went on for two years, until September 9, 1989, when a wildcat strike turned into a riot.

An early-morning mob of nearly six hundred angry people (mostly union members from outside the area) stormed a housing camp that housed nonunion workers. They pushed down the chain-link fence, turned over buses, and tipped over and torched several mobile homes. Locals were assured that the National Guard would be sent to help maintain law and order, but the governor's order never came and the troops never showed up. It was, in short, a frightening day of chaos in a normally quiet northern community.

That morning I woke to a friend's phone call from across the bay in Canada. "What's going on over there?" she asked. "There's a mushroom cloud of smoke above your town. Is your whole town on fire or what?"

We turned on the radio. "Don't go into town today," the mayor warned. "Stay home and stay safe."

Mary sitting on the edge of Rainy River in 2003. Credit: From the archives of Mary Casanova. Reprinted with permission.

I knew that very morning that someday I would have to write about what we'd been living through. As a writer, I would someday have to make sense out of the unthinkable. How could a fight over jobs turn so violent?

Fortunately, many of the nonunion workers had been ordered to leave their housing camp before the attack, leaving only a few guards left to defend the empty mobile homes. A few individuals were hospitalized, but fortunately, no one was killed. And when it was all over, numerous protesters were charged with felonies.

Five years after the event, when I was working on the novel, I had to discuss with Charlie the threats I'd been hearing about. "It's one thing for me to write about what happened," I said. "As a writer, I need to do that. But it's another thing entirely to put our entire family at risk by writing this book. What do you think I should do?"

He looked me in the eye. "I know you'll write it as fairly as you can. Go for freedom of speech."

And so I wrote the novel through the eyes of twelve-year-old Bryan Grant, whose father is his hockey coach and who is getting increasingly involved at the strike site and through late-night protests of vandalism against "beakers" and "rats"—the names they gave the nonunion workers. By writing this novel, I stepped back into all of the emotions I experienced when the actual riot took place. I relived my own fears and anxiety and outrage that something like this could happen to our town.

When the novel finally came out, seven years had passed since the actual event. Fortunately, time heals. Many locals told me that the story gave them a way to talk about what happened with others. "It brought it all back," I was often told. "I remembered right where I was when the riot broke out." When *Riot* was nominated for a Minnesota Book Award, locals seemed to start viewing the book—and me—as feathers in the town's cap, much to my surprise. Though I'd been white-knuckled about the release of the book, I quickly realized that the book became part of the overall healing of our community.

Because the wounds in International Falls over the labor dispute didn't heal quickly, I knew I couldn't wrap the story up with a big red bow. Some issues simply cannot be tied up so neatly. Instead, the reader is left to ponder how Bryan and his dad move forward from the jail scene, to ponder how his family picks up the pieces in the months ahead, and to ponder how the town moves on. I hope that the novel leaves readers with a willingness to ponder how each of us—given the right conditions—could turn angry. Anger is part of being human. It's what we do with our anger that matters.

CURSE OF A WINTER MOON

"I know it sounds crazy," I told Charlie one day, "but I think there's a story calling to me in the south of France."

"C'mon, be honest," he said. "You just want to take a vacation there."

"No, really! I'm being honest."

In the middle of January, Grandpa Max stayed with our kids for two weeks while Charlie and I went to Provence (the south of France) so that I could research and write *Curse of a Winter Moon*. Not only was I delving into a story set in another country, but I wanted to write a story set in the 1500s. Where did this story come from?

The easy answer is that a story was nudging at me, waiting to be told. But there are two other strong influences: my interest in wolves and my experience of living through a riot.

When I was researching wolves for *Wolf Shadows*, all my research took me back as far as the Middle Ages, when people truly believed in were-wolves. As recently as the mid-1500s in France, authorities could tell if you were a werewolf, or *loup garou*, through several alleged methods:

1. If the accused had rough palms, it could mean that person had been shaving his or her palms to disguise his or her true identity
2. If the accused had bushy eyebrows that met in the middle
3. If the accused showed up one day with many bruises that he or she had not had the day before, it could mean he or she had been out running with the wolves the previous night
4. If the accused had symptoms of epilepsy

We took the TGV trains from Paris to Provence, the south of France, where I set *Curse of a Winter Moon*. Credit: From the archives of Mary Casanova. Reprinted with permission.

5. If the accused was born on Christmas Eve
6. and so on...

When I learned that thousands and thousands of people had been burned at the stake because of such alleged evidence, such superstitions, I felt the need to know more about those times. I was haunted by a question. How could such fears lead people to commit acts far more horrific than the monsters of their imagination?

My interest in wolves led me to doing research, and research on wolves led me to beliefs about werewolves, which led me to the 1500s in France. Also, living through a labor dispute that turned violent, and having witnessed the polarization of a community and eventual mob behavior, compelled me to want to understand the attitudes of a distant time when fellow humans could treat their neighbors with similar fear and hatred. Researching and writing *Riot* and *Wolf Shadows* led me to write *Curse of a Winter Moon.*

Setting, for me is critical. I must be fully engaged in a setting in order to be fully in my main character. After all, character is the engine for story. Though many writers will say that character comes first, I find that when I start experiencing a setting through my character's senses, I start to truly know who they are. What do they see in a given situation? Does he notice the broad sweep of a slate sky or the soft petals of

My research in France consisted largely of using my five senses. We wandered through numerous villages outside our base in Aix-en-Provence. I wrote down names from monuments and cemetery stones that fit the region and time period. I breathed in the air, took in the mountains and clear streams, sipped coffee in outdoor cafés, and tried to imagine life hundreds of years earlier on the same cobblestone streets. One day we drove to Roman ruins outside one village and left our tiny rental car and climbed to the top. We looked down on a small graveyard, on vineyards and fields. Magpies flew past. The sun was pale and cold. Bare trees rattled like old bones. I lingered to soak in the setting for the eventual scene, where Marius and his little brother, Jean Pierre, climb the ruins (Chapter 4). Credit: Charlie Casanova. Reprinted with permission.

a decaying rose? What interests him? What is the mood of a place when filtered through a particular character's state of mind? When I write, setting and character are inexplicably interwoven.

In *Curse of a Winter Moon*, Marius is charged with his mother's death-bed wish to "take care" of his little brother, Jean Pierre. But taking care of his brother isn't easy, especially when his little brother was born on Christmas Eve, a day largely believed to indicate one's destiny to become a werewolf, or *loup garou*. Marius isn't sure what to think of his own brother. He both loves him and fears him. But in a time of great political and religious upheaval (the Reformation), Marius tries to protect his brother as best he can.

Books were so rare and valuable in the 1500s that they were most often owned by nobility or clergy members. But times were changing. More people were learning to read and were wanting to read. During the Reformation, many people were burned at the stake for reading the wrong book at the wrong time (the ruling church of the time, the Catholic Church, had lists of banned books). Also, if individuals were caught reading the Bible on their own without the guidance of clergy, they could be arrested for heresy, also punishable by death at the stake.

Ironically, this novel has received censorship for two main reasons:

First, the title has the word "curse" in it. This has led a few librarians in conservative communities to worry that they'll get complaints about the book and so will avoid potential complaints by not ordering the book. A form of censorship.

Second, there's a question of werewolves. Some educators and parents believe the book shouldn't be touched because it raises the question about whether or not Jean Pierre is a werewolf. However, the book truly isn't a horror story. There is not a real werewolf to be found in the book. It's a horror story set during a turbulent and dangerous time in history, and it raises important questions about religious freedom and the freedom to read.

When I researched and wrote *Curse of a Winter Moon*, I had no idea that we would soon be hosting an exchange student from France. When the edited manuscript was returned from my publisher, Christine Charles was there to read it through and give me her feedback. Credit: From the archives of Mary Casanova. Reprinted with permission.

In the writing of *Curse of a Winter Moon*, I became more aware than ever of the dampening affects of censorship. After its publication, I have been reminded that censorship continues in many forms. Though we have come a long way as a society in both our freedom to read and in our abundance of books, we should never take our liberties for granted.

MORE HISTORICAL NOVELS

The Klipfish Code

Minutes after our plane touched down in Oslo, Norway, I took a taxi with my husband and son to the Resistance Museum. Few Americans seem aware that Norway had been occupied by Nazi Germany for five years during World War II, and this stop at the Resistance Museum was just the beginning of my research on this subject. My heritage is Finnish, Polish, Swedish, and Norwegian. Traipsing from Oslo to the western shores of Norway, I felt comfortable with the culture of this country. With blonde hair and blue eyes, I felt right at home. The fjords and ocean inlets, the mountains and islands, however, far exceeded the landscape of northern Minnesota in grandeur. I absorbed the setting with my senses, hoping to find a story set in this Norwegian landscape.

In my reading about the occupation, I came across a little-known fact. When the teachers of Norway were ordered to teach their students Nazi philosophy, the teachers unanimously disobeyed. In response, the Nazis hit hard. They rounded up one out of every ten teachers (about one thousand) and shipped them off to concentration camps. To make an example of some of the teachers, the Nazis crammed five hundred teachers into a boat and, in slavelike conditions, shipped them north along the western coast of Norway to a concentration camp. The German boats followed the teacher-filled boat, which was used as a bomb finder.

My Norwegian sweater, much like the many sweaters my grandmother once knitted. Credit: Courtesy of Terry Nagurski studios. Reprinted with permission.

To help research a story set in Norway, I had to go there, home to some of my ancestors. 1) Farmlands on Runde Island; 2) Mary on Runde Island; 3) Mary stepping off the train in Andelsnes; 4) Charlie, Eric, and Mary in the fjord region of western Norway; 5) Alesund, with its busy harbor life. Credit: From the archives of Mary Casanova. Reprinted with permission.

While I roamed from museum to museum, from island to island, and learned of countless heroics by ordinary citizens, I was haunted by questions. How would I have reacted to living under a Nazi occupation? Would I have been as brave as many who risked their lives to win back Norway's freedom? What kind of choices might I have faced? To explore my haunting questions, I needed to write a novel. Originally, the story was titled *Sliver of Light*, but I have since retitled it *The Klipfish Code*.

The Klipfish Code (Houghton Mifflin, 2007).

When Nazi Germany invades Norway in 1940, Marit Gundersen's world is turned upside down. She and her brother, Henrik, are sent to stay with her grandfather and aunt on Godoy Island, but not even the island is safe during the occupation. Marit resents her grandfather's unwillingness to stand up to the Nazis, until she's faced with her own dilemma of rescuing a fallen resistance soldier and carrying out his mission, which puts the lives of those around her at risk. It's story that underscores that in war there are no easy answers and a score of heart-wrenching choices.

The Red Skirt's Girl

Years ago, I spoke at a writers' conference with one of my editors in Grand Forks, North Dakota. After we finished speaking, we sat at a table with my agent and my husband, discussing the conference and sipping wine.

"What do you think you'll write next?" my editor asked.

I told her about a slice of history from my region that had been haunting me for a few years. She scribbled down bits of the story I proposed on a cocktail napkin, which I have since learned she's kept in her office drawer now for ten years!

Now I'm starting the novel. Some stories need time to incubate, but this one has taken forever. I think I was waiting to catch up in my craft as writer to take on this subject material. *The Red Skirt's Girl* is definitely for young adult readers. I have written a few chapters and my editor wants more, so I do hope that before another decade passes I'll have a book in hand to share with readers.

Here's the bit of history from the early 1900s that first captured my imagination and started my usual question-asking and pondering. The excerpt is from a recorded incident from *Koochiching*, by historian Hiram M. Drache:

> *A true event, which became the basis of a long-standing joke about the early days [ ] occurred when on of the "girls" got drunk and on her way home fell on the sidewalk and froze to death. . . . The local pranksters had taken the frozen corpse and stood it in the corner [ ] of the hall where the meeting was held. Needless to say, it caused a great stir for the early part of the meeting. Shortly after that event a local attorney . . . headed a group who desired to clean up the town and build a school and some churches.*

Ever since I read this excerpt I have been haunted by this frozen prostitute. How did she really die? What was her story? Who, as a joke, stood her body up in the community hall? I have wanted to vindicate this woman's life, a woman who lived in a time and region where women

My home in Ranier dates back to the turn of the century. The people in the photo outside what is now my home have always made me wonder about their lives: affluent people in a frontier village. Credit: From the archives of Mary Casanova. Reprinted with permission.

had little voice and power. And though I feel anger for her treatment and sadness for her fate, my hope is that the novel I write will be about avenging this woman's life—and about the redeeming power of love.

With every new project I'm filled with a healthy respect and fear for the process ahead. What if I can't do this subject justice? What if I'm trying to tackle something bigger than I can handle? What if I fall flat on my face? This next novel stirs up all of those familiar fears and questions, which means I just might be on the path toward writing a story that matters and a story that readers can't put down.

All I can do is try. I won't know until I get a draft, revise it endlessly, and get the eventual book into the hands of readers. Time and again, I remind myself of my author-friend Jane Resh Thomas who always says, "Just do the work."

Books with Dolls

CÉCILE: GATES OF GOLD

I was on the road at the end of a long season of school visits and conferences, ready to slow down for a few months, when my agent contacted me about a possible opportunity with American Girl. As requested, I called Tamara England, the editor of a new series, *Girls of Many Lands*, to discuss what she was looking for.

"I just finished reading your novel *Curse of a Winter Moon,*" she said, "and I loved it." She then said she hoped I would be willing to write a story for American Girl set in France sometime during the long reign of King Louis XIV. It would be part of a book-and-doll series about girls from distant lands and time periods. "We're asking award-winning authors," she added, and indeed, I eventually joined up with authors such as Laurence Yep, Chitra Banerjee Divakaruni, Kirkpatrick Hill, Jane Kurtz, and others in a series of novels aimed at girls ten and up, each accompanied by a nine-inch collector's doll. Each doll would be dressed appropriately for her time period and culture and would provide a tangible "taste" of that culture. My character, Cécile, for instance, wears an embroidered silk gown and light blue mules on her feet. She even carries a small feathered fan.

Initially, I was skeptical about writing a novel with a commercial slant to it via a doll. Would that force me to compromise creatively or to write something less literary? "Do I get to find my own story?" I asked. "I wouldn't be able to write a novel with a predetermined plot."

Tamara explained that the story would have to comply with the normal constraints of a series, such as word length and age appropriateness—and that the main character had to be a girl. But yes, she assured me, I would have the freedom to write my kind of story.

Though I had looked forward to returning home to a quiet summer and relaxing after my busy travel season, I didn't want to pass up this opportunity. "Yes. I'll do it."

Indeed, not only did I find a story I was passionate about writing, but I discovered that the Cécile doll has added another dimension to story creation—that is, a physical expression of character. The doll, which today stands proudly on my studio shelf with the rest of the "Girls of Many Lands" dolls, has helped bring Cécile to life through cultural and costume details. She is an extension of the story, and not the

Mary and Cindy Rogers, fellow writer and former teacher of French, sipping coffee in a café in the town of Versailles, right outside the palace gates. Credit: From the archives of Mary Casanova.
Reprinted with permission.

other way around. And that matters to me. Plus, a doll is simply lots of fun.

As it turned out, the deadline for delivering the first draft was extremely tight—months away instead of years. I knew that to write this novel I would have to go to the palace of Versailles, and the sooner the better, so that my subconscious could begin working on the story. I called a writing friend, Cindy Rogers, whose former life included teaching high-school French.

"Cindy," I said, phone in hand, "I have an offer for you. I have an amazing opportunity to write for American Girl, but a very short time to produce the first draft. I need to get to Versailles as soon as possible. Would you be willing to join me and help me get around since my French is so limited? I'll pay your way."

The courtyard was expansive. When I first arrived, I took a few deep breaths and reminded myself to stay open, absorb everything around me, and trust that the story would come. Credit: From the archives of Mary Casanova. Reprinted with permission.

About a week later, we were walking down the ancient cobblestone streets of Versailles, some thirty miles from Paris; and I started the transition to a time long ago when only horses and carriages clattered along. We checked into our hotel, napped to catch up with the time change, and finally emerged to begin seven days of exploration of the palace and its grounds.

Stepping through the golden gates of the palace and across the cobblestone courtyard made me shiver. I didn't know how I would find my story, and the thought of grasping an important time in history and getting all the details right nearly fueled a full-fledged panic attack. But fear wouldn't help me out. I knew that. Instead, my job was to explore, to stay open, and to listen for the story that called to me.

I had already learned that King Louis XIV found himself threatened as a child in the original palace in Paris. Surrounded by feuding nobility, the young king and his mother left Paris and were in self-imposed exile until he reached the age of fifteen. He dreamed of building a palace outside of Paris at his hunting estate at Versailles.

Eventually, with the help of many thousands of workers and at a hefty cost to the French people, the palace was built out of swamplands.

Known as "the Sun King" because life at court revolved around him—much as planets revolve around the sun—King Louis XIV held power by keeping the nobility dependent on him. The king was the center of all palace life, and only by gaining favor with the king could members of the nobility get the lands, titles, and wealth they desired. In this way he held power until his death at age seventy-seven.

Daunted by the long-ago king's power and by the palace itself, I wondered how I would find a story that could reach the hearts and minds of girls in modern-day America. The life of women at court was interesting, but it wasn't a life I would have wanted. These noblewomen were subject to endless rules of etiquette, and they led a life that revolved around card parties, dances, gossip sessions, theater, and music. There were rules, all based on royal birth, about who could stand and who should sit in a room at one time. And women's concerns were considered to be of little consequence at court, unless one was the queen or maybe the king's mistress. For instance, a queen or princess, even if pregnant, had to tolerate long bumpy rides to hunting estates if the king happened to want to hunt. Princess Marie-Adelaide, King Louis XIV's granddaughter, believed she miscarried because her concerns about a long trip went unheeded.

As resplendent as palace life looked from the outside, the realities of court life were unappealing to me. I couldn't imagine living in such a hornet's nest of a class system, and I couldn't identify with a girl growing up in the court. Finally, I decided to write about a character I *could* identify with—one who grows up in the country and has little in the way of material wealth.

Cécile is good with animals and appreciates nature. One day, when a royal hunting party gallops by, she catches a runaway horse that has dumped its rider. The rider, sister-in-law to King Louis XIV and referred to as "Madame," rewards Cécile with a place at court as a servant to her six little dogs. And yes, they really did have servants whose sole responsibility was to care for dogs of court members.

Palace life is not what Cécile had imagined it to be. In many ways, life is easier: for example, she isn't hungry all the time and she finally has decent clothes to wear. But in other ways, she finds that life is far *more* difficult than she could possibly have imagined. She learns that new gowns and a full stomach are no protection from the dangerous complications of court life. When a measles outbreak threatens the king's family, Cécile risks everything by joining other servants to defy the court doctors—and thereby saves the king's great-grandson, who eventually becomes King Louis XV.

Cécile: Gates of Gold is filled with historical characters that I tried to get to know as best I could by combing through history books, memoirs, and personal letters written at that time. Madame really did fall from horseback twenty-eight times. The king did have doctors whom he trusted with nearly absolute power over his health and life. And a governess and her nursemaids did play a heroic role in rescuing the infant Anjou from the barbaric methods of the court doctors when a measles epidemic hit. It was the bravery of these seemingly powerless women that helped me to find my story. They risked everything by going against the court doctors and barricading themselves and the two-year-old prince in the closet until his fever passed. They could have been sent to the Bastille for their actions, yet they chose to do what they believed was right, no matter the consequences.

This was a piece of history I'd never come across before. If it fascinated me and captured my admiration and my heart, then maybe it would be of interest to others. Eventually, the story spun out like a complicated web, and I sent off the initial draft on time to my editor. After revisions and precisions, the book and its accompanying doll both came to life. The book told the story and the doll showed my character in court finery of the sort a peasant girl could only dream of. I continue to receive passionate e-mails from girls and women about the novel and how it speaks to them today.

One of the aspects of working with American Girl that impressed me was that I had a whole research department at my disposal. When I found the exact breed of Madame's dogs elusive (Were they King Charles spaniels, Papillion, or Continental Toy spaniels?), I e-mailed one of the researchers, who dug deeper and helped me sort through sometimes conflicting information. Not only did the staff help me with small details, they also provided me with extra resources, from Web sites to history books. I'd never had the sense before of being part of a team when it came to researching a novel. I loved it. The staff cared as much as I did about historical accuracy. Every detail had to be backed up. Every part of the story had to be plausible for its exact time and place in history. I owe American Girl's research staff a debt of gratitude.

After the book was released, I returned to France with my editor. We spoke together at a writers' conference and at an International School in Paris. We also spoke at a writers' conference in Brussels, Belgium, where one of my former exchange students, Evi Rubbens, met up with us.

Also joining us in Paris was the cover illustrator of *Cécile*, Jean-Paul Tibbles, from Sussex, England. He spoke about using his daughters as

My American Girl editor, Tamara England, helps show the painting of Cécile to an appreciative audience in Paris. Credit: From the archives of Mary Casanova. Reprinted with permission.

inspiration for the portrait of Cécile, and Tamara and I talked about our author-editor process. Then we unrolled the original oil-on-canvas painting of Cécile in the Hall of Mirrors. It is at least three feet by five feet, and was met with appreciative ooos and ahhhs from the audience—because Jean-Paul is really, really good. He's been commissioned to do a portrait of the Queen of England. He's also the illustrator of the Josefina series with American Girl.

Later Jean-Paul told me to take the illustration back home with me to Minnesota. He said that if he kept it, it would just end up in some dusty corner of his studio. "Just take it?" I repeated, stunned by his generosity.

When Tamara and I boarded our plane back to the States, I carried the rolled-up painting under my arm (very carefully) and returned to Minnesota. I had the painting framed in a faux gold gilded frame. I shared it by hanging it in the local coffee shop for a few months with a written explanation on how I'd been given the painting. Now it hangs in my husband's State Farm insurance office so anyone in International Falls can stop by and see it. Someday, maybe I'll donate it to our local library or perhaps to the Kerlan Collection of Children's Literature in Minneapolis. But then again, I'm not sure I can part with it. After all, like the chance to write *Cécile* for American Girl—the painting, too, was *a gift.*

What could be more satisfying than signing books with my friend Jane Kurtz, author of *Saba,* another title in the Girls of Many Lands series. Left to right: Jane and Mary at American Girl Place, New York City. Credit: From the archives of Mary Casanova. Reprinted with permission.

JESS

One of the unexpected gifts of working with an editor is that sometimes incredible friendships form. Such has been the case with Tamara England, who seems to know how to bring out the best story in me. So when she called and said she had another project I might be interested in, I was all ears.

For the past few years, American Girl has featured a "Girl of the Year" doll and novel. The eighteen-inch doll is available for a limited

Hiking in Belize along the Mopan River. Credit: From the archives of Mary Casanova. Reprinted with permission.

time—one year only—though its accompanying novel remains in print longer. Tamara said they were thinking about an adventurous girl who is also a traveler, and felt that I would be a good author to write the story. Of course! I was more than happy to work again with Tamara.

In addition to the broad concepts that Tamara provided when she approached me, she and I went back and forth with e-mails and phone calls about the story's *who, what,* and *where*. As far as *when,* she'd already explained that the "Girl of the Year" story is a contemporary story. We discussed a possible archeological dig that my character might go on. But where? South or Central America? Egypt? I researched possibilities, as did the staff at American Girl. Finally, we settled on Central America and the country of Belize.

The day after we dropped our youngest, Eric, off at his first day at Macalester College in St. Paul, Charlie and I flew off to Belize for research. Much as I had set off in a hurry to France to research *Cécile,* I found myself once again on a plane, armed with travel books and a focused itinerary. Charlie, who has become my capable research photographer, was quite happy to join me.

We touched down in heat that never let up. After hopping a crowded bus from Belize City, we settled outside of San Ignacio at a bed-and-breakfast establishment, aptly named "Iguana Junction," for two nights. Green iguanas of all sizes lounged in the overhanging canopy of branches along the nearby river. Chickens roamed freely around the three outdoor dining tables while we ate meals that included fresh pineapple and papaya.

From there, we met up with our guide, Patrick Warrior. Patrick was an imposing man, not just because he carried his machete with him wherever he went, but because he was tall and square shouldered. He explained that he was a descendant of native Mayas and of former African slaves from Colonial Belize. His skin was deep brown, and his laugh thundered around evening campfires.

Patrick Warrior, our native guide, kept us on the move (and safe) in the jungle. Credit: From the archives of Mary Casanova. Reprinted with permission.

And he carried his machete, he explained, not only to help clear the vine-covered trails, but also to protect us from poisonous snakes and such.

I had arranged with Patrick before leaving for Belize to meet with a Maya family, to canoe or kayak, to explore caves, and to climb ruins. Patrick made sure that we did everything on my request list, and remarkably, about 95 percent of what I experienced firsthand ended up in the novel.

Again, setting is so important to me in discovering my characters that I truly could not have written *Jess* without going to the jungle. I had to experience things firsthand, or *first foot*, as was the case when fire ants swarmed and attacked me when I stepped on their pathway!

It's Jess's first time out of the country with her archeologist parents. It's her first time being home-schooled. And it's her first time traveling without her older brother and sister. She anticipates that her trip will be a great adventure. And it *is*, but not entirely as she envisioned it might be. Her adventure isn't just about kayaking, or about exploring the Maya ruins. It's also about making friends with a local girl named Sarita and discovering how their lives are similar and different. When she and Sarita stumble upon a yet-undiscovered cave of valuable Maya artifacts, Jess also comes to appreciate her parents' work in trying to protect such treasures for future generations—especially when the cave is threatened by looters.

As I experienced Belize, I tried to maintain a childlike wonder about this foreign land. Evidence of poverty and a different way of life from mine was everywhere—half-finished construction projects, bony dogs and horses, and houses that looked more like huts. Yet I was struck, as I met and talked with locals, by how the people of Belize were rich in other ways. Parents boasted about their children's educational accomplishments. Despite the common practice of washing clothes by hand, children trotted off to school every day in clean uniforms. Families hovered around kitchens, chatting and laughing. I wanted to convey some of these discoveries through my story.

One night, Patrick left us with our tent on a sandy peninsula in the cavernous Rio Frio cave. He lit a candle in the sand, then climbed back out over the toothlike boulders of the cave's mouth. Water roared around the peninsula, echoing off the cave's cathedral-like ceilings. Before tucking in under flimsy sheets in our pup tent, we made giant shadows on the cave's wall as candles glowed and flickered. Do I use that experience in the story? Absolutely.

Another afternoon we pushed our canoes through a narrow passageway into a different cave, the Barton Creek cave. Stalagmites and stalactites formed shapes on both sides of us as we paddled deeper and deeper into the mile-long cave. Bats whooshed over our heads and squeaked from the cave's ceiling. Clusters of bats hung at eye level on the cave's walls as we paddled deeper. In the water below, we shone our spotlights on colorless blind crayfish. And a type of colorless scorpion clung to the rocky wet walls. The cave created its own music—a steady, rhythmic drip-drip-dripping. When we turned off our lights to experience utter darkness, I experienced an unexpected music. Stein, another visitor to Belize, had joined us that day, and she began to sing in Danish. Her voice rose high, clear, and angelic. We were rapt listeners.

Later, she said, almost apologetically, "I just couldn't resist singing inside this cave." It turned out that she used to tour with a youth choir around Europe and sing in all of the largest cathedrals.

And that's how I came up with the idea to have Jess's new friend, Sarita, sing in the cave when they're paddling together. And of course, Jess's reaction is similar to my own reaction to the experience: awe and gratitude.

I had the opportunity to visit with a Maya family who had chosen to live by "the old ways." Rather than moving into town, they lived in the jungle and cooked on a wood-fired clay stove. They raised and ate their own chickens, did all their wash by hand, and lived on very little. Without the cooperation of the Bol family, I would not have been able to write about a Maya family. I couldn't pretend to be an expert about how everyone lives in Belize, but I could study one family and try to capture their chosen lifestyle as authentically as possible. They were generous, answering my many questions. And they were eager to share something else: the cave that they had discovered several years ago on their property.

As the sun was setting and the jungle shadows deepened, Mrs. Bol led us in her flip-flops and sundress over a high ridge and down a winding path to the other side. She stopped beside a grate-covered black hole that went straight down.

When I was too scared to crawl on my belly through one tunnel, Charlie, my husband and travel photographer, wasn't. Credit: From the archives of Mary Casanova. Reprinted with permission.

"This is what my husband found one day," she explained, "when he was out hunting with his dog." She started down the makeshift ladder first, and then welcomed us after her. "Watch your head."

I really wasn't sure about this. What about snakes? Scorpions? Tarantulas? Weren't those good enough reasons to skip this part of the research trip? But I wasn't going to be left behind in the darkening jungle, so I followed. She showed us the cave as her husband had found it. Her flashlight illuminated an endless array of ceremonial bowls, dishes, and daggers (used long before in human sacrifice ceremonies). She showed us two skeletons, thought by experts to be nobility from

(Left) Our guide, Patrick, took a moment to kick the soccer ball under the gaze of the Carocol ruins. (Center) Research huts at the ruins of Carocol. (Right) Reproduction friezes at Xunatunich ruins. Credit: From the archives of Mary Casanova. Reprinted with permission.

another Maya era. Finally, she pointed to another hole in the floor of the cave. "That leads to a storeroom."

Charlie looked interested in climbing down into the tunnel and in on his belly. I wanted to—I really did—but I just couldn't muster up enough courage. "You tell me what you find," I said. I waited instead for him to come out, dusty with the reddened earth. "Lots of stuff on shelves in there," he said. "Definitely a storeroom."

That was another experience I decided to use in the story, but I had to draw on my imagination and Charlie's description rather than my *own* direct experience. Thank goodness for imagination! And for an editor who can help shape such experiences and imagination into a coherent story.

In short, writing *Jess* was a grand adventure. I started with a ten-year-old girl who would learn something from her *own* grand adventure. Along the way, I discovered something about Maya culture, history, and archeology in the process. I learned about the dangers and beauties of jungle living. I wandered around the ruins of Caracol and its archeology camp. And I learned that I could face up to some of my deepest fears, including hunting tarantulas by flashlight, and rise above them, (well, almost). I hope that when young readers step into Jess's story, they'll catch a glimpse of another world through the eyes of a character much like themselves.

MORE BOOKS WITH DOLLS

I'm often asked, "Will you do more books for American Girl?"

"Do you have another doll coming?"

The answer is: Wait and see.

Working with American Girl has been a pleasure through and through. Not only have I had the chance to work with an extraordinary editor, but I've also been able to lean on an amazingly resourceful research department. When I needed help, for example, finding current-day names for girls in Belize, the research staff supplied me with over a dozen names to choose from.

I've appreciated that my concern for accuracy is mirrored in every aspect of creating dolls at American Girl. Jess comes with accessories appropriate to her time in Belize: a passport, a backpack, a macramé hanging swing, an inflatable kayak, a moped, and more. She's true to the story. Because, after all, it's the story that always comes first.

More dolls?

I certainly hope so.

LAUNCHING DOG WATCH

I had just finished writing a novel and was emotionally tired. I wasn't ready to jump into a novel with weighty issues right away. "Maybe I need to work on something light next," I said on the phone to my agent, Andrea Cascardi.

"Well, have you ever considered writing a series that follows three or four characters, something aimed more at second-, third-, and fourth-grade readers?"

"Hmm. That's something I've never thought about before. Let me think on it."

Within hours, I started to imagine the dogs of my northern village starring in a series. I had always wanted to write about Ranier, where dogs are allowed to roam free. And this is true. At the village clerk's office is a big book called *Doggie Mugshots.* In it, each registered dog of the village has its photo, description, and perhaps an anecdote about it. In return, the dog is given a registration tag to wear on its collar, and then it is allowed to roam the village, as free as any citizen.

The catch is, however, that if a dog gets in trouble it will get a sticker on its page. Too many stickers will mean that the troublesome dog will have to stay home, tethered or fenced. Or, if the dog is a biter, it may end up being banished completely from Ranier.

Why not use my own two dogs, Kito and Chester, in a series? Here they are, doing what they do best: begging in the kitchen. (Kito, left; Chester, right). Credit: From the archives of Mary Casanova. Reprinted with permission.

I had always wanted to capture this unique dog system—and where better, I began to think, than in a series.

Over coffee, my fellow writer Sheryl Peterson and I brainstormed for a title to the series proposal I'd typed up. We listed several possible titles, but when Sheryl said "Dog Watch," I knew that was it. Like Neighborhood Watch (or *Bay Watch*), the dogs' mission was to keep the village safe for people and dogs. Within a couple of weeks, Simon and Schuster agreed to a four-book series (with more books to be added).

My own dogs, Kito and Chester, with their own distinct personalities, seemed the perfect main characters. We had adopted Kito from the Humane Society when he was four months old and in need of a stable home life. He is part Chow-Chow and cautious by nature, and I wasn't sure if he was a full-grown dog or a puppy when I first met him. The sign at the kennel said "Free to Good Home, Call Humane Society." But rather than wag his tail and roll on his back when I approached, he stood his ground and growled. We decided to give him a chance and took him home.

Apparently, his upbringing had been pretty terrible. He was thrown from a car window on a cold wintry night with his siblings and was later found and dropped in someone's snowy backyard. From there he ended up at another home, where the mother abandoned not only Kito and her other dog, but her two kids as well. That's when Kito landed with the Humane Society for the second time.

Now, a few years later, he still watches anyone a long time before warming up to them. He seems more of a thinker, so I decided the story would be told through his point of view. Furthermore, I figured if any dog in the village could read, it would be him. In the series, he reads discreetly by firelight when no one is looking; he is a reluctant leader when the alpha dog, Tundra, is unavailable; and he has a terrible fear of strangers.

Chester, on the other hand, is a dorky but loveable beagle, both in real life and in the book. When our son, Eric, mentioned wanting a beagle someday, I took it as my holy mission as a mother to find one and bring it home. En route back from a week of school visits, I passed a pet store that said "Puppies" in the window. I knocked on the door, as it was locked. The pet store worker willingly let me in, even though the shop had just closed, and allowed me to peruse the puppies. "Do you have any beagles?" I asked.

"Yup," she replied, and pointed to a cage at the back.

The sign above the cage said "Beagles," but the three emaciated, wiry, long-nosed creatures behind the metal bars barely looked like

Son, Eric, at eighteen, and his beagle buddy, Chester. (Left to right) Maggie, foster dog, Chester, and Kito, taking it easy on our living-room couch beside the wood-burning stove. Credit: From the archives of Mary Casanova. Reprinted with permission.

dogs. They yipped and scrambled at their bars, falling over one another. "How old are they?" I asked.

"Three months, maybe four."

I wondered if they'd been in a cage all that time. Visions of pet farms flooded my mind, and I didn't want to support buying from ill-respected breeders. But these puppies needed homes desperately.

I picked out the one with more brown and white patches. "That one," I said, and she pulled it from the cage. The puppy stunk terribly, and he burrowed under my neck as if his life depended on it. Maybe it did. Foolishly, thoughtlessly, but thinking of rescuing the puppy and meeting my son's wish, I plunked down $400 for the animal, which included his registration papers. Then I drove home, hoping the puppy could last the next two hours without peeing on my chest.

When I stepped inside my back door, Charlie and Eric met me, wondering what the "surprise" was that I'd mentioned via my cell phone. I set the scrawny, long-nosed beagle on the floor, and he cowered and pressed his body against the floor and under the edge of the cabinets. He slunk and slithered forward, and in horror, I realized that my guess was likely true. He'd probably never been out of a cage.

"What is it?" Charlie asked.

"A northern?" Eric mused, referring to northern pike, known for their long snakelike bodies and snouts.

"A rat?" guessed Charlie.

"C'mon, guys, he's a beagle!"

We gave him a bath, dewormed him (our vet had never encountered a dog with so many worms ... and used the word "spaghetti" to convey the quantity), and took him into our lives.

Chester now bays at full tilt when any dogs go by. He goes on "benders" when he can, our word for when he gets on the trail of anything interesting and follows it until he drops. He snores terribly. And he really does sniff the ground so loudly that his snuffling interrupts normal conversations.

Kito, wiser and more staid, tolerates Chester in his own way. Together, they spend their days lounging on couches while I'm writing, protecting me from possible dangers, and providing a wealth of inspiration as the main characters for the Dog Watch series.

One of our former dogs, Gunnar, a basset hound, also plays a significant role in the series. Before he was, sadly, struck by a car, the greatest risk of running free in this village of 199 people, Gunnar made the rounds daily at his favorite haunts. He loved stopping by Ed's Marine to take naps in the back room with Ed. He stopped by various homes where kids knew him by name, and these kids reported later to me that he once ran inside and jumped in bed with a child's sick father. He took shelter at another home until a storm passed. He allegedly mistook cattails at one house for hot dogs. His favorite places to hang out, however, were the two pubs: Woody's and the Ranier Municipal Liquor Store. More than once I had to fetch Gunnar from "the muni" and haul him home, despite his reluctance to leave. "You can't take him," one man at the counter mumbled. "He hasn't finished his p-pizza." Gunnar often came home long after we were in bed, usually after 1:00, when the two pubs closed. He'd howl or bark

Gunnar, the inspiration for the basset hound in the Dog Watch books, loved to visit everybody in our village, and more than once he came home from the tavern after it closed. When he woke us at 1:30 in the morning with his bellow outside the door, he'd step in and flop down. "You're grounded," we told him. Credit: From the archives of Mary Casanova. Reprinted with permission.

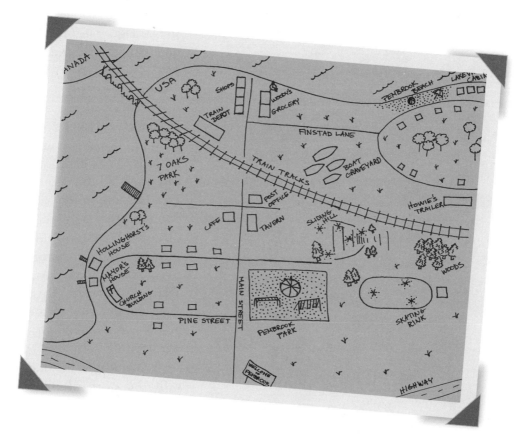

A map of Pembrook, based closely on the layout of Mary Casanova's village of Ranier. Credit: Sketched by Kate Casanova. Reprinted with permission.

at the back door. We'd leave our cozy bed, let him in, and he'd flop on his dog bed. More than once, we told him straight. "You're grounded."

As a fiction writer, sometimes the lines between reality and fantasy become a bit blurred. I've likely imbued my dogs with more intelligence than they actually possess, but then again, who knows? Maybe not. I mean, what do those Ranier dogs talk about every day when they gather at the fire hydrant outside the post office?

BOOK ONE: *TROUBLE IN PEMBROOK*

The first book in the Dog Watch series, *Trouble in Pembrook*, establishes the setting—a tiny northern village called Pembrook where dogs are allowed to run free; the story's premise—the dogs are working behind the scenes to keep the village safe for people and dogs; and the characters—Kito, Chester, Gunnar, Tundra, Schmitty, Muffin, Lucky, and others. The plot is simple. There's trouble brewing with vandalism around the village, and on top of that, the alpha dog, Tundra, has gone missing. Someone—or something—is up to no good, and the dogs must stop them before it's too late. In Book One, Dog Watch is formed when the dogs all put their noses together and decide to work as a team.

I couldn't be happier with the work of illustrator Omar Rayyan for this series. He captures the dogs' personalities in cover art illustrations, and his interior black and white illustrations are whimsical and energetic.

Early sketch for interior illustration, Dog Watch, Book 1: *Trouble in Pembrook*. Illustrated by Omar Rayyan. (Aladdin/Simon and Schuster). Reprinted with permission.

Aimed at readers ages seven to eleven, the series is meant to be fun, readable, and only slightly scary. For instance, when I initially brainstormed for plot ideas for the various books and suggested "kidnapping" to my editor, she steered me toward a lighter tone. "How about dog-napping?"

BOOK TWO: *DOG-NAPPED!*

Dog-napping *is* deadly serious for the dogs of Pembrook. First Muffin and Missy disappear, then a box of puppies, and then Willow (the dog that Kito and Chester both have a crush on). Dogs disappearing is alarming, and the dogs work together to find the missing dogs before more vanish.

Book One is set in summer, Book Two in fall (with a spook house and Halloween playing into the eerie setting for the disappearances). By the story's end, the dogs do indeed get to the bottom of things. And, as is true of the general tone of these stories, real evil isn't generally behind the problems. The resolution is usually accompanied by a greater understanding of Pembrook humans or dogs. I might be writing from a dog's point of view, but the things dogs care about the most are pretty much the same as what we care about as people: a safe place to call home and staying close to those who love us most.

Reading the newspaper at home with Chester. Kito, however, is the only dog in the Dog Watch series who can read. But he keeps it to himself, because "smart is one thing, but show-offy is another." Credit: From the archives of Mary Casanova. Reprinted with permission.

BOOK THREE: *DANGER AT SNOW HILL*

Book Three: *Danger at Snow Hill* is set around Christmas. When trouble erupts at the sliding hill, the dogs are accused of doing things they are not guilty of, such as getting into garbage cans and attacking sledders. A new village resident decides it's time to see that all village dogs are locked up at home the way they are "in the rest of the civilized world." Kito and Chester and the others need

In Book Three, Chester and Kito are hot on the trail of a trouble-making intruder. Here, in real life, they're exploring the mysteries of their backyard. Credit: From the archives of Mary Casanova. Reprinted with permission.

The settings for Book Three are the ice rink, warming house, and sliding hill of Pembrook. Credit: From the archives of Mary Casanova. Reprinted with permission.

to find out who or what is behind the trouble—a bear, a wolf, what?—and rid Pembrook of the nuisance before they lose their freedoms forever.

BOOK FOUR: *TO LURE A BURGLAR*

Book Four: *To Lure a Burglar* delivers what the title promises. The Big Fish/Great Lure contest is just around the corner, and Pembrook villagers have been working on their homemade wooden fishing lures. The trouble is that someone's stealing the lures from under the dog's noses. Not even Tundra was able to stop the burglar. "What's a dog worth," she asks, her tail and head drooping, "if it can't guard its own home?" She quits as alpha dog. The rest of the dogs must catch and stop the burglar if they ever want to hold their heads high again—and if they're ever going to get their real leader back!

BOOKS FIVE, SIX, AND BEYOND

Due to the initial popularity of the Dog Watch series, I have been asked to write more stories about the doge of Pembrook. Once again, I do not have to look very far for inspiration. It's all around me in my quiet, little northern village that Kito, Chester, and many other free-roaming dogs call home.

Picture Books

THE HUNTER

The doorbell rang at 11 p.m., and we opened the door. A tall, wiry young Chinese man stood on our doorstep. The middle-aged man at his side thanked us for temporarily hosting Hui until his Rotary exchange program across the border in Canada could untangle unexpected diplomatic snags. "It will only be a week or so," the man assured us as he helped bring Hui's large bags into our living room, and then drove away to cross the border into Fort Frances, Canada.

Our kids were in fourth grade and first grade at the time, and I wasn't sure that we were the best family to provide even temporary housing for a high school student. But Charlie was the Rotary president in International Falls back then, and he thought it could be a good experience for us as a family. "Okay," I agreed, "if it's only for a week."

One week soon turned into two, then three, and with school starting up and no sign that the Canadian government was easing up on its restrictions toward China that year, we enrolled Hui in the International Falls high school as a senior. He ended up spending the school year with our family (the first of four exchange students to live with us in the years to come).

When Hui moved in with our family, he knew very little English. He carried around a handheld translating gadget to aid in learning English. He

When Hui came to live with us from China, he knew little English. To practice his English, he told us a few Chinese stories, including the story about a heroic hunter named Hai Li Bu (*The Hunter*). Here, beside our woodpile, Hui, age seventeen, and Kate, age ten. Credit: From the archives of Mary Casanova. Reprinted with permission.

returned one day from high school and said he'd discovered the best word in the world. When he was in a circle of friends in the hallway and everyone was talking and he didn't understand everything, he found one word he could use in all situations.

"Oh? What's that?"

"Whatever," he said, with a big smile.

As he worked on learning English, I suggested he share Chinese stories with us so we could learn more as a family about his country and culture. He shared several stories, but the one that captured my imagination was about a hunter who has a terrible choice to make. I asked Hui if he would also translate the story from the book of Chinese folktales he'd brought with him, and wrote down the bare bones of the story.

The story is about a hunter named Hai Li Bu, who provides for his village as best he can, until a drought comes. At the turning point of the story, Hai Li Bu has to decide whether to flee and save himself, or sacrifice his life to save his village from impending disaster. Faced with the hardest of decisions, Hai Li Bu looks at the villagers and asks, "Do you want me to die so you can believe?"

"But you ask us to leave our homes," a village elder says. "How can we know what you say is true?"

Hai Li Bu studies the villagers, "young and old, more splendid than jewels," and determines that "he could never allow them to be destroyed." He tells them the magical source of his knowledge, and as he does, before their eyes, he slowly turns to stone. Finally convinced, the villagers flee before the impending storm and flood destroys their village. When they return, they find Hai Li Bu "in his stone

As a writer, I try to slow down in a story's most dramatic moments and get as close as possible to what's happening within my main character. Similarly, at the point when Hai Li Bu struggles to make a heart-wrenching decision, Ed Young seemed to "zoom in" closer to his subject, close enough to show us the tear in Hai Li Bu's eye. Credit: Illustrated by Ed Young. (Atheneum/Simon and Schuster). Reprinted with permission.

prison" and "with many hands, and many tears carry him to what remained of the top of the mountain."

"If only we had not doubted him," the people said. "If only we'd listened."

My challenge in retelling the story was to look beyond the bare bones of the story and consider what the villagers learned, which is why the story is bookended with the theme of listening to one another. What did they learn, I asked myself. They learned to listen to one another. And that's where, as a storyteller, I fleshed out the story by introducing in the opening that when a drought came, "worst of all, the villagers began to argue and stopped listening to one another." The end of the story reinforces this idea: "And to this day, somewhere in China still stands the statue of Hai Li Bu, who gazes upon his valley below, where the villagers listen to every person, including the youngest child."

Hai's original telling of the story haunted me for its allusions to my own Christian teachings about Christ's emphasis on living as a servant, even to the point of sacrificing his life for others; about the woman in the Old Testament who turns to stone when she doubts the warning to look back at her burning city; and of course, about the flood in the story of Noah and the Ark. Most importantly, the story of the hunter spoke to my own beliefs that true leadership is about serving others, which is perfectly demonstrated through Hai Li Bu's selfless yet difficult decision.

I credit Kendra Marcus, my agent at the time, for believing in the soul of this story and for pushing me to flesh it out and bring out in relief the story's most poignant moments. She sent the story around and it kept coming back with rejections, some of which were very nice, such as "Love the story, but not quite right for us," and such.

One day, a call came from Simon and Schuster. They were very interested in the story, but only if Ed Young would illustrate it. They felt they needed him, with his well-deserved Caldecott medals, to help "carry the book." Unfortunately, I was told, they didn't think that Ed Young was available for years.

Oh well, I thought. Another nice rejection. At least someone enjoyed the story as much as I did when I'd first heard it. Within the next day or so, however, Ed Young apparently stepped into the offices of Simon and Schuster, read the manuscript, and agreed to take it on. I think he must have dropped everything to work on it, because he had the illustrations done in less than a year.

The Hunter is truly a collaboration. It's a story that's been around for hundreds and hundreds of years in China, and I would never have known about it if Hui hadn't shown up one evening on our doorstep. Ed Young, born in China, took the story a step further by giving the story an elegance that I couldn't have imagined. I understand he used a branch dipped in black ink to create many of the illustrations in the book, which were on display for a time at the Chicago Institute of Art. The final book is a work of art. I truly am honored to play a part in bringing this ancient, beautiful story to life.

When I share this story with kids, I often ask them how it makes them feel. They answer "Sad." "But happy, too," they'll say. And when I ask them if they think that Hai Li Bu made the right decision, they unanimously agree. "And do the villagers learn anything from the hunter's sacrifice?"

"They learn to listen to one another."

A few years after the book came out, Charlie and I drove to Winnipeg, Ontario, where Hui was doing graduate work after earning his college degree in China. I showed him the book and he exclaimed, "Mom, this is amazing." He shook his head in disbelief. "It's a *miracle*."

So many opportunities come our way in life. We can open the door to unexpected knocks, not knowing what will step into our life. Opportunities bring uncertainties, heartache, and work. They shift us uncomfortably out of our routines. But opportunities also have the potential to bring into our lives more joy, more understanding, more love. I'm thankful that a knock came on our door years ago, and though I almost declined the opportunity, we opened the door and Hui stepped into our lives.

ONE-DOG CANOE

Every summer for the past fifteen years, I've met with other children's writers and illustrator's on an island on Rainy Lake. For a week we work on our own manuscripts and gather in a circle in the evenings for group critiques. Over the years, I've gathered a wealth of knowledge and insight from this group, which has included Jane Resh Thomas, Marion Dane Bauer, Marsha Chall, Barbara Santucci, Janet Lawson, Lisa Westberg Peters, Phyllis Root, Catherine Friend, Sheryl Peterson, Alice Duggan, Kitty Baker, Lois Berg, and Amy Ehrlich.

During the day, we also take time to swim, hike, read, and canoe. On one such afternoon, I was canoeing with Phyllis Root. Usually we stay on Mallard Island, but that year it was unavailable to us as a group, and we instead stayed on nearby Jackfish Island, home to the former Dahlberg estate. Bror, the resident cocker spaniel, thought he should swim after our canoe as we explored the channel.

Mary, paddling in pajamas around Mallard Island one early morning in August. Credit: From the archives of Mary Casanova. Reprinted with permission.

"He's too far from shore," I said. "He could get hit by a boat or drown."

So we paddled to a rocky shoal, waited for Bror to catch up with us, and when he did he shook his sausage body, getting us all wet, but happily climbed into the canoe and took up his post in the center. On we paddled.

We came around another bend, and there at the end of a dock, staring at us forlornly, was a golden retriever. I knew from the dog's woeful expression that if he could talk, he would have asked, "Can I come too?"

I stretched out my arms. "No way," I said. "It's a one-dog canoe!"

Then I glanced over my shoulder at Phyllis. "One-Dog Canoe. That could be a picture book, couldn't it?"

We rhymed and played with word possibilities as we paddled on, and when I returned to the cabin I was staying at, I wrote down the first draft. Many, many drafts later—thirty-two, to be exact—I had a publishable manuscript and an interested editor at Farrar, Straus, and Giroux.

Bror, the cocker spaniel who swam after our canoe and inspired the first draft of *One-Dog Canoe* in 1996. Credit: From the archives of Mary Casanova. Reprinted with permission.

Melanie Kroupa is a terrific editor. She cares about every word, every nuance of meaning, every detail of a story. The first illustrator she found for the story had done covers for *The New Yorker* magazine, and his work samples were stunning. I agreed that he would be perfect. But after three or four years of waiting for him to finish the artwork, he suddenly shipped all of the nearly finished artwork back to Melanie and wrote that he could not complete the project. Life, apparently, had gotten in the way. We waited for months, hoping he might change his mind, but he didn't. He'd figuratively bailed out of our canoe.

Finally, Melanie discovered a new talent in Ard Hoyt, fresh out of art school. I love that Melanie often runs ideas and artwork past me, asking for my input. Editors rarely do that with authors, and I appreciate being included in the process. We both wanted an illustrator who could capture the natural world with a blend of realism and whimsy. Ard Hoyt's artistic sensibility was perfect.

I'm often asked if I get much say about artwork. With *One-Dog Canoe*, early in the process, I sent Ard slides of northwoods' wildlife and landscapes. When his early sketches came back, I loved them! But I was concerned that the girl looked too old, more like ten than five. Her legs and arms, especially, seemed too long in the first sketches. Melanie took my concerns to Ard, and he adjusted the girl's limbs to convey a more age-appropriate character.

One-Dog Canoe is very autobiographical for me. What child doesn't want to spend time alone with Mom or Dad? I, too, had always wanted to have exclusive time with one of my parents, but I don't remember ever having time alone with either of them. I would hop in the station wagon to go to the grocery store with my mom and think, "Wow! It's

Ard's illustration of the crowded canoe brings back memories of piling into a station wagon with my nine siblings, dog, and parents to head north to the cabin. Credit: Illustrated by Ard Hoyt. (Farrar, Straus, and Giroux). Reprinted with permission.

just me and Mom!" But before she could leave the driveway, the back door of the house opened and out ran one, two, three, or four brothers. They'd wave their arms and say, "Stop! Wait! Can I come too?"

No wonder this story, then, is about a girl and her dog setting off on an adventure, "A trip for two, just me and you," only to have countless others join in—uninvited—on their fun.

In earlier drafts, the girl in the story would actually say "No way!" or some such to the animals. But my agent commented that if the child says "no," and then nobody listens, the story goes against the "Just Say No" campaign at that time, empowering children to set boundaries. That's when I realized that I hadn't been great at saying "no" or setting boundaries—as a child or as an adult—up until that point. I had been well schooled in "being nice" and not hurting the feelings of others, which made it difficult to speak.

In *One-Dog Canoe*, the heroine becomes increasingly frustrated with her growing crew that doesn't heed her hints that "we're pretty darn full," or "maybe next time," etc. Yet the overflowing canoe is, in large part, her problem because she doesn't say "no." When the story turns disastrous, (as the reader expects with similar picture books, such as *The Mitten*), that's when the girl must choose how she's going to handle what went wrong.

Beaver steps forward and says, "Sorry, we should have listened to you. Guess you were right, it is a one-dog canoe."

Rather than scold and reprimand, the girl makes the most of the situation and says, "That's okay, we had a good swim." She forgives and moves on. And then, in a spirit of cooperation, they all work together to bail out the canoe. The animals help set the girl and her dog off and on their way again.

Ard Hoyt, illustrator of *One-Dog Canoe*, *Some Dog!* (2007), and *Utterly Otterly Day* (2008), lives in Benton, Arkansas. Credit: From the archives of Ard Hoyt. Photographer: Sonya Sones. Reprinted with permission.

Sharing *One-Dog Canoe* has been a joy. I love to see kids smile and laugh when I present the story, and it's equally satisfying to see adults have the same childlike reaction. When I visit schools, I often bring puppets along and have children help enact the story as a skit, stepping up to the microphone with a moose or frog to ask "Can I come too?" With someone narrating, it's an easy and fun story to act out with kids of any age.

SOME DOG!

What could be better than working with Ard Hoyt on *One-Dog Canoe*? Working with Ard on more picture books!

Some Dog! is about a basset hound named George. He has a good life with his owners and takes things "slow and steady, steady and slow" and "smells a thousand scents on the wind." But when a stray arrives, a spry little dog that can do tricks and puts George to shame, the man and woman take the stray in and call him "Zippity." George sinks into depression, until a storm hits one night and Zippity tears in crazy circles and finally runs out the door and into the stormy, dark night. George doesn't mind. But when his owners press him to go find Zippity, George reluctantly relents. Using his strengths, his nose and his

When a local shopkeeper asked me to ride in a *One-Dog Canoe* float in the Ranier parade, how could I refuse? (Mary, left, and Shirley Ettestad, owner of Rainy Lake Gifts, in 2003). From the archives of Mary Casanova. Reprinted with permission.

steadiness, George finds and saves Zippity from sinking into a "swampy, murky mire." When the two dogs come home, George realizes that he never really lost his place in his family, and accepts Zippity, even sharing his bed at the end.

Though the story features dogs, it's really about sibling rivalry and what happens when one child feels displaced by another. George can't compete with Zippity, and in his insecurity, he retreats into himself. But George has talents and strengths that Zippity lacks, and when he steps back into himself and saves the day by doing what he does best, he's reminded that his family loves him, just the way he is.

That said, this story grew in my imagination from an incident that happened between two dogs. My sister and my parents each had a golden retriever from the same litter. Dakota is an all-star athlete with boundless energy and zest for chasing balls down hills. Bucky, on the other hand, is a less muscled dog who likes to move more slowly and appreciates his dog bed more than exercise. When Dakota went to stay

In *Some Dog!* (2007), George is "slow and steady, steady and slow," and life is perfect until a little dog named Zippity comes along to outshine George. Selected illustration from *Some Dog!* By Mary Casanova, pictures by Ard Hoyt. Text copyright © by Mary Casanova. Pictures copyright © by Ard Hoyt. Reprinted by permission of Farrar, Straus and Giroux, LLC.

for a week at Bucky's house, all I heard from my mom was how amazing Dakota was. "He jumps from the dock and catches the ball in the air!" she said, going on to list many other amazing tricks that Dakota had impressed them with. "He's some dog!" But all I could think of was their own dog, Bucky, who could never match his brother's stamina, athleticism, and outward talents. That's when *Some Dog!* was born in my imagination.

UTTERLY OTTERLY DAY

Utterly Otterly Day is the third book illustrated by Ard Hoyt. The title has been in my mind for half a dozen years, and every time I watched otters play off the end of our dock or slide across our half-frozen bay in the winter, I wished to write an accompanying picture book. But what would it be about? Since I had always loved the playful nature of otters, I decided to try to convey their antics in a story. But how could I convey the playfulness of otters through language?

Once, when Charlie and I were canoeing with Gunnar, our basset hound, we paddled around a peninsula and heard a light pattering in the thicket. Just as we turned to look at the shore, we saw three baby otters chasing each other down the path, straight into the water. They dove in as our canoe slipped by—one, two, three—almost into our canoe! Our dog was slower to catch on to what had just happened, but as their heads popped up in the water, he went crazy, bellowing and turning in circles until we nearly toppled over. We paddled on, delighted by the baby otters. Could I use that in a story somehow?

In *Utterly Otterly Day*, Little Otter loves to play. When his explorations take him too far from home, it's Sister Otter who warns him that Cougar is dangerously close. Little Otter manages to escape with his sister and Mama and Papa, and together they all return to the safety of their otter den.

In earlier drafts, I went back and forth with my editor, Kevin Lewis at Simon and Schuster, about the story's ending and its implied theme and settled on what I'd come to realize in my own life. We all make mistakes. We all need plenty of grace. We need one another. So rather than a harsh scolding and a *Peter Rabbit* ending, this is how Little Otter's day draws to a close:

> He tucks tail to nose.
> He needs his family—
> no matter how big he grows.
>
> Then Little Otter closes his eyes
> and dreams in a sleepy otter way
> of his whippedy, slippedy,
> swishily, swashily,
> dizzily, whizzily,
> warily, scarily,
> utterly otterly day.

This is a preliminary sketch that Ard Hoyt did as he started brainstorming for his artwork for *Utterly Otterly Day*, scheduled for release in 2008 by Simon and Schuster. Credit: From the archives of Ard Hoyt. Reprinted with permission.

THE DAY DIRK YELLER CAME TO TOWN

On a recent trip to New York City to visit with editors, a story came to me in the middle of the night. I woke at midnight to the title, *THE DAY DIRK YELLER CAME TO TOWN*, and the opening lines that included "the wind curled its lip and the tumbleweed stopped tumblin' along." A fairly light sleeper, I generally try to leave my imaginative work for the daytime, but this was different. I decided to get up. Charlie was sound asleep beside me, so to avoid waking him, I took my notepad into the bathroom, closed the door, and wrote down the lines in my head, a general idea of the story, and the ending. Then I went back to bed, suspecting that it would all look like rubbish in the morning.

But in the morning, the title and phrases looked curiously promising.

I fleshed out a rough draft on my laptop, then headed off to my appointment at Simon and Schuster to meet with editors. When Kevin Lewis told me that he was looking for more stories that showed boys as rough-and-tumble yet that they could be readers, too, I said, "I think I have a story for you, but I should probably do a few more drafts first."

The story fell into my head like a gift. In short, Dirk Yeller is a famed outlaw who is looking for "something or someone" to ease his restless mind. The townsfolk of Cowtown scurry when he steps through a door, but when the outlaw has exhausted all his options: the post office, the general store, the sheriff's office, and the saloon ... and is left standing alone in the town's dusty streets, it's a child who steps forward. The child recognizes a bit of himself in Dirk Yeller's restless ways, and suggests the new place in town—the library. Sure enough, Dirk Yeller steps in and begins to turn page after page. At long last, he's found something to ease his restless mind—an endless supply of books. And ever since that day, the library has been the busiest place in Cowtown, "especially for curious, restless folks, like Dirk Yeller and me."

There's a lot of Dirk Yeller in me, too. That restless, active kid in me is still alive and well. I, too, need to focus my high level of energy into something productive. Though I love to be physically active (hiking, horseback riding, cross-country skiing, etc.) I am grateful that I discovered along the way that a good book could hold my attention. I've been writing for children for nearly seventeen years now, and writing never ceases to challenge my creative and intellectual skills—to ease my restless mind.

Finally, this picture book is also a way to say thanks to long-gone Andrew Carnegie, who made huge financial donations to help establish libraries throughout the United States.

• • •

In all these ponderings and musings about my life and my stories, I hope you've found something useful. A colorful thread. A button. Perhaps a comfortable shirt, much like one of your own. Something that helps us connect as writer and reader.

I love a famous quote by Mother Theresa: "In this life we cannot do great things. We can only do small things with great love." My life has been filled with blessings and adventures, challenges (or "learning opportunities"), and small accomplishments. As I journey on, I still hope to write books that matter— stories that kids can't put down. I hope to listen to the stories that call my name, to settle down at a blank page, and to once again—begin.

Index

About the Author

MARY CASANOVA is an author of picture books and novels for older readers. Her award winning books include *The Hunter* (illustrated by Ed Young) and *Some Dog!* (illustrated by Ard Hoyt). Mary enjoys the out-of-doors and lives near the Canadian border in Rainey, Minnesota.